YOUR LIFE IQ

Natalia Alexandria

Published by

www.NataliaAlexandria.com

ISBN: 978-0-578-13810-7

DEDICATION

To all those choosing to live a fulfilled life.

ACKNOWLEDGMENTS

I am grateful for the many who inspired and supported me with my vision for the future. Special thanks to Victoria Pearson, Mari Tankenoff, and Silvia Garretson, all of whom contributed to the production of this book.

TABLE OF CONTENTS

FOREWORD

YOUR LIFE IQ is based on a lifetime of personal experience, research, and study in the subjects of behavioral sciences, mind-body and vibrational medicine, philosophy and spiritual traditions. This book not only relies on the knowledge of experts, scientists, and other great thinkers, it also evolved from my individual circumstances and experiences. These events created a unique mindset that imposes specific attitudes and philosophies which can hold true for us all. This mindset is a gateway to powerful living.

Born in the spring of 1958, I was raised in New York City by Eastern European parents who survived World War II. Amongst two siblings, I was the middle child—generally overlooked—except for my physical attractiveness. I was neither the prized first child nor the boy and the baby. Instead, I was left to fend for myself emotionally and was handed the role of strength—a role with built-in expectations for me to endure and survive. Taking the challenge head-on, I became tough, resilient, and determined. My parents deserve high praise for their insistence on many extracurricular activities, including the study of music and art. I attended private schools, enjoyed the richness of two cultures, and was put on a path grounded in tradition.

My professional life began on Wall Street in the securities industry. It was a fluke. An employment agency sent me on a job as an assistant that paid better than any other job I had had. I set no goals, but quickly moved up and became a trader of equities and options. Later, I worked as an institutional broker. Wall Street was a place coated in money and power, and those privileges made my life exciting and fun. The world's door had opened and the possibilities were endless. I flourished in this type of environment and hungrily seized all opportunities. My artistic side blossomed, and I created a fine arts company that operated in New York, Paris, and Budapest—and provided the chance to live in Europe. After those experiences, I became a marketing consultant, specializing in strategy and new business development. During that time, I moved to Miami and took my life circumstances and passion into the writing of both fiction and nonfiction books. I became a certified life coach. Although I never married and had no children of my own, there has been no shortage of rich experiences, both in love and with children.

Did the preceding incidents *train* me as an expert in life? Not quite. There was another, less pleasant side to my preparation. My life was also riddled with adversity before I became thirty years old. One week after my fifteenth birthday, my father committed suicide. At nineteen, I was hospitalized with a life-threatening illness. At twenty-three, I was sexually assaulted. By my mid-twenties, a congenital visual disorder was beginning to surface. At twenty-eight, my visual problem was irreversible. I had Stargardt's disease and was legally blind.

Disillusionment and sheer pain sent me into the depths of introspection. I traveled there frequently, but continued my quest for solutions. Tenacity began to weave into the tender fabric of my soul. As I went forward, I dared that deep dark place to destroy me and unleashed my ability to be obstinate. Amid all the upheavals, I still possessed a fierce desire to survive, a belief that anything was possible, and an iron will. The strong Natalia took care of the vulnerable Natalia, and I became extremely protective of who I was and what was positive about me. That protective shield would have to become stronger. As best I could, I integrated a variety of disciplines for my body, mind and spirit.

By the time I was in my mid-thirties, I had probably absorbed several libraries of books, magazines, and newspapers. I began to notice a lot of overlapping information about the body, mind and spirit. There were some common messages, but specifically through life experience, certain things became very clear to me: Conditioning—particularly perspectives imposed by those who influence us—parents, teachers, friends, and society—could strangle many aspects of living and success. I was relentless in my quest to make sense of it all. Despite optic migraines, I still read (mostly audio or skimming through printed material with visual aids) and explored all topics—and the more difficult, the better. I would understand everything, even if it killed me—since nothing already had. Through my incessant study, I picked up more disciplines. Over time, I began to notice marked improvements in all aspects of my being.

By then, I started to unravel how it was that I was surviving a visual limitation without perceived limitations. In a remarkable irony, my lack of vision became my saving grace. Strangely, this visual problem was one where I was blind in my focusing ability. All I had to rely upon was peripheral sight. That meant I couldn't see details, was constantly disoriented, and had to figure out a way to maneuver energies from other areas of my being, in order to *appear* normal. Happily for me, my initial response was denial—I refused to believe that I was limited at all and bypassed the option of crawling into a hole to rot. Instead, I resorted to *seeing* peripherally, which was always stressful, but I refused to give up. Oddly enough, I was being forced to *see* things from a big picture point of view. Thus, the alignment of the energies of my body, mind and spirit, began to take hold. I discovered miraculous living.

As I meticulously connected the dots, a holistic framework sprouted. Adding, subtracting, adapting, and changing—had been my middle names and held the key to why these disciplines were working. The result was nearly forty years of testing, experimenting, and weeding through information using common sense—what works, and what doesn't. Although multiple life crises had threatened to throw me off course, I knew I didn't have the luxury of postponing *real* solutions. Perhaps that was why I had to experience such hard punches. But my desire to make a difference by contributing all that I possibly can, and a vision that had always matched the size of the universe, has invited the wonder that I call life.

Here, I present *YOUR LIFE IQ*. I hope that it will bring new perspectives, insight, and inspiration to how you are now living. May we all bring the best of who we are, day after day, into the remarkable experience we call life.

Your Life IQ

I.

THE PHILOSOPHY

At last—a life-changing guide that works. *Your Life IQ* considers all of who we are: body, mind and spirit. The tactic is holistic, not fragmented or halfway. It is not a temporary solution, but an energetic shift in consciousness that will produce a meaningful and happy life. This methodology relies on a big picture approach of balancing your unique energy system to function at its optimum. The core of this powerful philosophy is based on the innate intelligence that exists within each of us—an intelligence—that allows us to successfully navigate our lives. Whatever your dreams and goals, *Your Life IQ* will invigorate your life and produce miraculous changes with simple, common sense principles.

This book is a *new* approach to self-improvement in the Twenty-first Century. Times have changed, and so have our lives. Today's world is bursting with high-tech inventions and complex information. It is a fast-paced environment of multi-tasking—stressful and competitive. There's too much to do and so much to know. Who can keep up? How do we manage our challenging lives while being driven in so many directions? How do we accommodate all that is demanded of us and still find balance and equilibrium?

Your Life IQ ploughs through these challenges by awakening the most positive forces from within you to align body, mind and spirit. It is all about discovering your untapped resources of energy that provide the ability necessary to attain the life you desire. Finally, it is about cultivating the best of who you are, day after day, to produce the highest quality of life experience.

We've all got it—an inherent intelligence that acts as a power source to propel us in the right direction. And just like our IQ or EQ, it too, can be improved. Whether intellectual or emotional, intelligence is measured in several ways, and can be applied to how well you make decisions in your life. However, since your life IQ is natural and comes from within, we must learn how to access this precious resource by breaking through the many filters of our conditioning. It's the moment when we begin to question and evaluate if what we believe in our life should be reconsidered. Or, perhaps we're changing, and we need to learn something more. Once this intelligence is accessed, this special resource unveils your essential qualities—the qualities that make you distinct from all others. It is an exceptional source of energy that inspires us to take action, and when discovered and utilized, your life pursuits can be realized successfully.

There are many ways to measure intelligence, such as processing, reasoning and communicating information. Our life decisions and choices must be approached in a similar way. If navigated efficiently, we move through life with an approach that fills us with ease, and allows us to flourish and thrive—particularly during difficult moments. Do you ever notice how much you struggle when confronted with a problem? There is an element of time and speed associated with our ability to problem solve. The more difficult the problem, and the more unfamiliar we are with that problem, the more we need to rely on our life IQ. This inherent skill affords us knowledge when facing unfamiliar challenges. It guides us through our inexperience by imposing those "gut" instincts that insist how to get through life crisis. It inspires us with novel thoughts and procedures, so that we are able to choose the right information—even if we are clueless. Imagine what it would be like to access this knowledge twenty-four hours a day.

Throughout our lives, we contribute a special essence to all that we do, but are you aware of its magnitude and impact on your success? This life-changing guide outlines a framework for life fulfillment that begins with you as an individual—the complete you. We can no longer ignore the caretaking of the entirety of who we are as human beings. The process of developing your life IQ unleashes your inner core, a place where equilibrium awaits you. We have all been equipped with an internal compass that can direct us in every aspect of our lives. Your compass is as individual as your fingerprints, packaged into a unique system of abilities, talents, goals, and dreams. Your essence is like no one else's, and once you unravel this inner core, a magical awareness will unlock the power to consciously create the life you desire. All aspects of living will exude confidence and strength to enhance and magnify your life experience.

Whatever your walk in life, it's a level playing field out there. Whether you are the CEO of a multi-national corporation, or struggling to put food on the table, whether you are famous or anonymous—we all have bodies, minds, and spirits to take care of. We have good and bad experiences, we have love, and we learn and grow. Regardless of circumstances, what will be your lasting imprint? Will you be happy? Do you think it doesn't make a difference? It does, and your presence on earth validates your importance as a participant. Will you take an active role, or allow others to maneuver your experiences?

This book also will explore the role of conditioning in your life, and why it can impede the success you desire. *Your Life IQ* will require an open mind, flexibility, and patience. It is a life-long commitment to never giving up, and a dedication to being the best you can ever be. This unparalleled process will reward you with remarkable realities that will produce countless victories and triumphs. To succeed, we will take practical steps and apply disciplines that will become as automatic as living and breathing—all to draw out our truest potential.

Born from nearly forty years of personal experience, research, and study in the subjects of the body (nutrition, health, and exercise), mind (psychology and mind-body medicine) spirit (Eastern and Western religions, metaphysics, and philosophy), this book is the bottom line to powerful living, a straightforward and sensible approach to quality living and life experience. It should be regarded as a starting point, as well as a supplement to achieving excellence throughout your lifetime. This is a one-stop reference guide to creating balance by discovering and using your inherent ability to navigate your own life successfully.

To increase your life IQ, we need to embark on a process that will trigger a shift in perspective to allow you to integrate the power of body, mind and spirit. It relies on certain information, certain disciplines, but most importantly, this book introduces a methodology that infuses common sense—which is why this framework can work for everyone.

Body is about your health and how you take care of the vessel that makes you efficient and energy driven. We will explore the basics of body health for you to determine your personal needs when considering body wellness. *Mind* is the way you integrate yourself and/or your work, and how you participate in society. Then, we will explore the perspectives that exist in the mind. Are they positive or negative in outlook and approach? What are the differences, and how do we improve? *Spirit* refers to the oneness with all that is living, and how you honor the driving force of your heart and soul. How do you honor who you truly are? And how does the integration of self affect your mission in body? We will discover how to balance our unique energy system—not someone else's—so that our body, mind and spirit work in concert to achieve your special idea of life fulfillment. We also will address the dynamic qualities of holistic energy and wellness, and why balancing this energy holds to key to extraordinary living.

These energetic components breed responsibility to self, others, and the world. How you take care of the body, mind and spirit, determines the level of equilibrium and quality of experience in your life. If one of these components is not in good standing, it affects the others, making you out of "balance." Like the legs of a chair, if one is broken, the chair tilts or collapses. These energetic components all are sources of energy, and it is solely your decision to choose whether it is positive or negative, energy plus or energy minus.

These sources of energy must be unified or they will disperse, creating disconnection from the self. If this happens, good energy suffers and is wasted because it makes up for the disconnection, rather than working optimally. Unless there is balance, one thing always is offsetting the other. By nature, we are resilient creatures and we're built to handle lots of *offsetting*. However, without properly caring for body, mind and spirit, we operate at disadvantageous levels that generally are masked as discomfort. This discomfort can go on well enough for years—until an illness strikes.

All three components are SYNERGISTIC, meaning that each depends on the other, and all are interrelated. Western thinking has generally looked for specific, isolated reasons for problems and illnesses. The approach is fragmented. Such thinking tends to overlook other contributing factors that might well be responsible, if not the source of the problem. That is why an abundance of reading material, experts, and drugs exist. This is not to say that there isn't a need for specificity, but we must reprogram our thinking to a more holistic approach of integrating all of who we are when assessing a problem or illness. The good news is that with major scientific advances and globalization, Western thinking has begun to incorporate the wisdom of Eastern philosophy and its medicine. This wisdom functions with the understanding that body, mind and spirit all contribute to why we become sick, and unless we strive to view our problems from a holistic point of view, we will not solve what ails us. Also, we must understand that holistic wellness includes not only the dimensions of the body, mind and spirit, but external dimensions such as occupational, financial, social and environmental.

On the individual level, all three components of body, mind and spirit are universal forces that help us evolve and contribute to evolutionary impulses around the world. Simply, this means that all three components are sources of energy—powerful enough to make a difference in everything and everyone we encounter. Consider that all that we do over the course of a lifetime contributes to changes that take place everywhere we go. Every moment of the day, you are making an impact by your choices, and by the attitudes you exude. Do we follow, observe, participate, detach, or surrender and isolate? How do we know which way to go?

Our internal compass always will direct us, but we must be "tuned in" in order to use its clarity. *Your Life IQ* lays the groundwork for developing and maintaining balance in all three components—the entirety of who we are. Success, regardless of how we define it, equates to the pursuit of happiness with the highest quality of life experience. Within this powerful process, we're reaching for success in all aspects of our life. This compact book of common sense practices is a hands-on guide that can be used time and time again, and will help us stay on course as we pursue our life goals.

II.

BELIEFS & CONDITIONING

Anything is possible. Do you believe it?

What do you believe about life, people and the world we live in? What do you believe about yourself? When it comes to life and life choices, there is one very important thing to keep in mind and reflect upon frequently: Anything is possible. This phrase of positive vibration is an attitude of the spirit. It makes everyone smile just to imagine the possibilities. But do you believe it—do you live your life believing that what you want is possible?

How do beliefs and conditioning play a role when facing challenges? It helps to understand that conditioning is all that is learned. What we learn is influenced by family, friends, society, religion, teachers, and our experiences. These influences mold our beliefs. Beliefs affect our thoughts and feelings in the areas of interest, opinions, values, passion, and goals.

These factors drive our behavior, and therefore, our choices. No matter who you are, you have been making decisions according to what you believe to be true. You also have been exploring options to better your life. All along the way, your beliefs led your decision-making. Beliefs create a kind of trust of how life works. These beliefs create a coherent picture of our life realities. They also produce multiple boundaries that give us a type of confidence that confirms our choices. But what happens when our lives don't go according to our plan? What happens when we suddenly lose control over life circumstances and events?

In whatever you do and whatever you choose, you must expand into the thinking that there is no *right* way to do anything. There is no *singular* approach to any choice, unless of course, you are purposefully hurting others. This doesn't mean that you abandon your principles or responsibility about how you choose to make decisions, but it does mean that you begin to consider the rigid boundaries of your beliefs. Those boundaries are there, and when something in our life is not working, the search for solutions becomes complicated and outright frustrating. We spin in circles, and many times, cannot find answers. Unfortunately, there are no secret formulas to life and success, despite how many worthwhile books we can get our hands on. Why? There are far too many people, far too many circumstances, and far too many experiences that affect us individually, so that integrating a particular formula is at best, a guideline, but not a solution.

What does this actually mean? It means that there are millions of ways to approach life and decision-making.

Professionally speaking, for instance, you can decide to become a lawyer, a postal carrier, a salesperson, a doctor, or a sculptor. Perhaps you'll decide to become an actor or a superstar. Maybe you'll decide to do research that will take you all over the world. On the personal side, you can marry anyone of your choosing, remain single, or decide to remain childless. Or can you? Are you sure conditioning—and what you believe—hasn't played a role in your decision making? And are you aware that you may harbor beliefs that have held you back from what you truly want to live?

We all have a variety of options, particularly in the United States, but what undoubtedly kicks in to limit our thinking is our conditioning. Conditioning is what we were taught to believe, and it creates those deep-rooted voices stuck in your head that begin to say, "Well, I don't know if I should be an artist. I won't make much money, and it's too difficult to succeed in that profession." In the personal realm, those voices might say, "If I marry him/her, will my parents approve?" "What will my friends think?" "Is he or she from the correct social background?" Those voices may also impose so much fear that you panic about your age and rush to marry. These voices might also cause you to think, "I'm miserable with my life. I'm stuck in a bad relationship, my job's too stressful, and I can't change my life—I have too many obligations." Or, have you heard the most defeated voice of all, which says, "It's too late for me,", " I can't do anything about it," or "That's the way life goes."

How often do you want to speak up—but don't—because of an existing emotional pattern that probably got started somewhere in childhood? How often do you concede when you desperately are seeking approval? Are you a people pleaser? How often do you just go along with whatever your friends say, while busily struggling and wishing you had the courage to disagree? How often do you feel undeserving of a big dream, sitting astonished in failure, rather than acknowledging that you just don't feel good enough?

Some of you might now reply, "Oh, come on, that stuff doesn't matter anymore. We live in a day and age where opportunity and freedom of choice are available to everyone." Perhaps, but you don't know *exactly* what's available to you and how difficult it might be to attain, until you are faced with the conflict of trying. And there will be conflict. Conditioning will hinder your efforts by unveiling a mindset that is littered with limitations and discouraging voices. They are the voices of what you believe, and those beliefs influence your decisions. The quality of your choices will reflect what you believe, and if at all limiting or negative, what you want will be harder to attain, and possibly, may become unattainable. If opportunity and success were there for the asking, we'd all be happy, satisfied, and contented, without a care in the world. If you're lucky enough to have lived your life making decisions with the utmost clarity and integrity, we applaud you! However, no matter where we are in our ability to stand up for what we believe, life most certainly will test our resolve by presenting greater and greater challenges.

Will you survive?

Every single one of us has an individual essence— an intelligence—that influences, motivates, and sets a particular comfort level in all that we do. When we are not in balance, we become uncomfortable and plagued with thoughts that oppose the instincts that tell us how we truly feel. In other words, we are not being honest with our essence—that aspect of our being, that if ignored, will most assuredly invite dissatisfaction, discomfort, and unhappiness. It is critical not to cave into someone else's idea of what's right for us. **What is right for us is discovered over a lifetime.** In this growth, we experience personal evolution.

Besides our individual development, humanity as a whole is in an evolutionary process. Simply, this means that from decade to decade, from century to century, from millennium to millennium, we are changing, adapting, and learning. As we can see, many peoples, cultures, languages, and lifestyles exist, and there is no single correct way to live or do anything. History clearly demonstrates that change—particularly change of mindset—is inevitable. If there were one *best* way, we'd all be happily following that glorious path!

Some of us practice religion, some of us don't. Some of us work nine to five and in an office, some work half days and at home, and others do not work at all. Then there are those who assume that being married is more secure than being single, while others find marriage too constricting and limiting. We all make our choices. One choice over the other does not necessarily assure balance. Hopefully, while we walk the path of life, we are honest about those choices; this honesty is the one ingredient necessary in keeping all three components of body, mind and spirit, in balance.

We need to accept that since birth, *all* of us have been told how to think and feel, and have been conditioned into taking on what others thought was acceptable. Generally assuming the best of intentions, our parents taught us all they knew, and guided us to the best of their abilities. Some of us didn't even have that. Through a wide range of subjects, educators tried to inspire and direct us. Religious leaders defined our morality and spirituality. Like the force of a tidal wave, our society has flooded us with conditioning. It mass-markets celebrities, reality TV, and other homogenized versions of what we ought to be—and also dictates what will make us happy, emphasizing the pursuit of material wealth. Every single environment and person we have encountered throughout our lives has left an imprint of influence, and gave us perspective. Unfortunately, not all influences have been positive, and not all influences were *right* for us. What we need to remember is that all influences served to give us **perspective, which is merely a particular viewpoint**.

Conditioning is all that is learned, good and bad. However, our internal compass—our intelligence and essence—is capable of directing us through the endless array of perspectives bombarding us throughout our lifetime. Are we listening, and do we register what our internal meter is saying, or is the obtrusive noise of the outside world successfully smothering that elusive voice?

Conditioning starts off as preparation, telling us what we should want in life. It has the power to cement our beliefs. We may have had parents or teachers who encouraged discipline when we played sports. It could have been the sole ingredient to why we excelled in that sport, and decided to pursue a career as an athlete. Or, that lesson of discipline coated our mind, and when we finally figured out a vocation, we accessed our ability to enforce discipline to succeed. Maybe nothing made sense until we shared our dream with a stranger on the street, who praised its originality enough for us to get that dream started. Or perhaps, the words of a friend were what kept us from making a dreadful mistake in a loveless relationship.

Not all conditioning is problematic or life changing. Conditioning is a natural by-product of humanity when it is evolving and integrating change, wanting to better the world as a whole. So what's wrong with that? Nothing—provided you agree with *their* assessment. For our purposes, let's just say that despite the altruistic intentions of certain conditioning, we still must choose what we want and how we want to achieve it, particularly if we want to create balance in all aspects of our life. Your choices will have to become *yours*, not *theirs,* and that distinction will relinquish the pressure you may feel when considering what to do.

Regardless of the type of dream we may possess, **change and its uncertainty is a concept that requires embracing,** and is a necessary ingredient for increasing our life IQ. When we embrace an open and flexible approach to all that may come in our lifetime, most of which will be unknown and unexpected, we are given the privilege of endless possibilities and solutions. We take on an unwavering attitude. Although we may not know what to expect in any given situation and we recognize that fear might creep up to deter our dream, we forge ahead into the unknown. This fearless attitude manifests from our spirit and is better known as courage.

Since humanity changes as a whole, wouldn't it make sense that it begins with each of us individually? How is change enacted? Plainly, it is the courage of one person multiplied into hundreds, then thousands, then millions, of people who dare to imagine a new or different idea. In other words, when an idea broadens, and if the majority can accept it, it becomes the norm. Yet, this is an uphill battle, and it takes time. Generally speaking, human beings detest change and the sacrifice that it entails.

For instance, in the United States, women won the right to vote less than a century ago. It took time, courage, and relentless persistence to break down conventional thinking into the acceptance of what now seems commonplace. Women went on hunger strikes to make their voices heard. Men fought them with all the power they had, set in their notion of the secondary role of women, except for the very few men who maintained a broader perspective. In the Fifteenth Century, Leonardo da Vinci was ridiculed when he imagined people flying in airplanes. It took nearly five more centuries for the reality of airplane travel to become as normal as the buggy and horse.

We all can cite an era when absurd distinctions and intellectual abilities were determined by a select few. We are not here to judge or debate these pitfalls in history, but instead are here to encourage accessing your essence—your own innate ability to determine what is right for you. Are you making your own decisions, or are you allowing others to dictate? Which *feels* more comfortable? If any part of you is feeling pressured because you are going against your internal director, watch out! Unconsciously, you've just asked for a lifetime of regret. Why? When you're afraid, and choose to go against what you feel is truly better for you, your life becomes one of disappointments that create regret. Rather than attempting and realizing dreams, you travel down the road of missed opportunities and the toil of regret.

So, imagine that we all have an individual essence, a life IQ that has been thwarted by conditioning. Of course, everything is an issue of degree: How far do you tip the scale in terms of where conditioning plays a role, and where it does not? Is it any wonder that stepping into conflict about whom we are and what we'd like to do in life, becomes a troublesome expedition? We slip in and out of crises only to discover that we were busy doing what everyone else expected. Except for the lucky few, not many of us really know what to study in school, what sort of profession to choose, or with whom to partner during different stages of our life. Much of this indecision can be attributed to the bombardment of suggestions from everyone we encounter while growing up. Even if you think you have figured out the way, chances are those ideas will change over a lifetime. It's trial and error. So how do we get through it all? Three words: **break your conditioning**.

Breaking conditioning doesn't mean that you toss all of what you know out the window and ignore or abandon everything you were taught—although, it might very well be the best thing to do. Perhaps the only challenge you may have in your lifetime is to stand up to your mother or father. The process still requires breaking a pattern, a conditioned response in a particular situation that makes you uncomfortable. Breaking your conditioning takes you directly into discovering your life IQ, your essence—that internal compass that never will steer you wrong. Do you know why? Because as long as you follow what you believe is right, the responsibility ends with you. There will be no one else to blame for mistakes, or to thank, if you succeed. All of your experiences, good and bad, maneuver you to where you want to be. Know that it is a sacred process to be who you want to be. If, on the other hand, you choose what someone else expects of you, you will be busy battling with not only what others expect of you, but also, what you expect of yourself. The burden is monstrous. Should you cave into what others expect, you will be the only one who has to suffer the ramifications of that choice. Unfortunately, it will be someone else's *right* decision that causes your perpetual turmoil.

Do you ever think about it that way? There you are, knowing full well what to do, yet at the same time falling prey to what he/she or they are advising. Worse, some of us have to endure threats, manipulation, bribery, and other forms of coercion aimed at getting us to make **their** choice, which of course, is always packaged as being in **your** best interest. "Oh really?" one should ask. You've got everyone espousing the right way to do things, yet you are the only one who has the potential of being unhappy and miserable. Where will they be when conflict crushes your thinking and crisis erupts? Can they halt your misery? What is good for one person isn't necessarily good for another. Just because your father was happy working in an office does not mean that you will be happy with the same circumstance. But cut him some slack. He is just transferring something that worked well for him in his life, onto you.

Naturally, there are those who will shut down and pretend they did the right thing and made the right choice, despite the alternative their internal compass advised. Why? It's easier to rationalize and make decisions based on what others expect. It's harder to pay attention to the wisdom of your essence when it disagrees with the norm. These pretenders, who shut down, step into the thralls of denial where there is less conflict and pressure. They will still insist on believing that they can "handle" the ramifications of their choice. Good luck. It never works. No matter who you are, no matter what the problem, events will continually arise to remind you of the choice you truly desire. The failure to make that choice will continue to haunt you, until you feel so pressured, that there is no choice to make but the one that you originally ignored.

For instance, we all know about avoiding the prospect of breaking off a relationship, and the obvious emotional difficulties this will entail. So, do we focus on the difficulty and discomfort, or do we do what's right and alert our partner that our feelings have changed— and we want out? Or, do we stay in the relationship out of guilt or fear, even go as far as get married and have kids, and then wonder how all of the anguish and flux was created? What will you do then? Before you know it, the relationship spins out of control and becomes unnecessarily complicated. If only we had been true to ourselves.

What happens if you ignore the signals and don't break your conditioning? One of two things is guaranteed: You either will experience regret and/or a sense that time has run out for you—that it is too late to have what you want in life—or, you will shift the blame for not getting what you wanted to everything but yourself. Such issues, admitted to or not, will translate into anxiety, depression, and other mental stresses and physical illnesses. Does this sound like something you would like to invite into your life? Do you want this sort of imbalance, let alone complication?

When we were young, countless people told us what to do and how to do it. If we did not conform to expectations, inevitable insecurities began to form. As children, we were chastised by our parents, teachers, and peers. Some of us were ostracized and excluded. We quickly discovered how to blend in by replacing our true selves with well-designed masks for those who expected us to be one way or another. Perhaps our parents discouraged us from minor personal statements, such as wearing bright colors—simply because they felt that muted tones were more acceptable. Maybe we were told that our parents would be proud if we got higher grades, excelled in sports, or went to church on Sundays. As you can see, none of these things is particularly detrimental. But maybe, we were born liking bright and flamboyant clothing, could not achieve higher than average grades, and just didn't relate to the religious experience at church. Were we wrong to feel that way?

The answer is obvious, but what is not so obvious is that the mere insistence of our parents or peers—a simple grimace of disapproval—or a sense of suddenly not belonging, can be a powerful influence. Depending on the strength of our personalities and the degree of those early influences, we did our best to change how we really were in order to be accepted. Over time, that impulse to conform developed into insecurities. As adults, these insecurities formed our beliefs, and manifested into behavior that triggered automatic responses that did not reflect our true nature. Despite our best intentions, feelings of inadequacy developed, which then mangled our ability to stay balanced when choosing what was right for us.

Do not underestimate the power of conditioning. It is a desperate struggle to evaluate how our lives have been negatively influenced. What we want, and what we are taught to want, involves endless conflict and the unknown, versus familiarity and the known. Breaking conditioning means going against the tide of accepted and acceptable decision-making. It represents a battle, whether internal (fighting ourselves) or external (fighting others). The unknown, even if it is better for us, inspires enough fear to hold us back. Also, no matter who we are, there are boatloads of people who will hold us back—not because they don't want what's good for us, but because they are fearful, and their fear reinforces the conditioned response we know all too well.

These are simple examples, but imagine if you, like many people, experience worse circumstances, such as neglect, abuse, and negative reinforcement. The unraveling of extreme negative conditioning is no different than unraveling any conditioning, but may require professional therapy. Even well-meaning parents who simply don't take the time to set a proper example, or clarify their expectations, can leave their children feeling abandoned and unwanted. These feelings further fuel undesirable insecurities, which can also require the undertaking of psychotherapy.

No one is exempt when it comes to preconditioned responses. Perhaps you were the type of child who needed more reassurance and guidance, a child who didn't possess the centered personality necessary to hold its own against parents who weren't particularly nurturing. Perhaps your parents continually pointed out what they considered to be your weaknesses, not realizing the damage they were imposing. Or, you may have had parents who praised your every move to a point where your attitude is one of entitlement—and left you unprepared to deal with life's challenges. Know that our world is set up in a way where we all have to struggle with issues of conditioning.

The funny thing about present-day conditioning is that, essentially, it is a fallacy. If any of these influences and their originators actually were *right*, wouldn't that conditioning continually solve all our problems? **In truth, problems are quite subjective, and they require management over a lifetime.** Breaking your conditioning by investigating your beliefs will not quite extinguish your perceived problems. However, when crises arise, this previous evaluation will make you aware enough to understand the symptom and Its source. Then it is easier to disregard its influence when making a decision. You will be able to loosen the rigid boundary of that belief. Alternative thinking will blossom, and new solutions can be utilized to solve difficult problems. We are challenged all along the way. When we ignore the need to be ourselves and stop questioning the power of our conditioning and what we believe, anxiety, depression, compulsiveness, and other illnesses can creep into our seemingly tranquil lives.

Conditioning and conditioned responses create energy shortages in our life, especially when our true self wants something different. We begin to spend too much time and energy debating between what is considered *normal*, versus what we truly want. Our good energy turns negative because we are stuck in ambiguity. Energy is drained and wasted, particularly when we are caught up in the downside of what we want. However, this energy can turn positive when we believe that we can have what we want, and begin to spend time exploring the possibilities. Consciously, we choose to focus on options that will bring us closer to that goal. We need to avoid the dangerous seesaw of negative energy replacing positive—it will certainly throw us out of balance.

Whatever we do, we must accept that it is our choice, despite the fact that we may feel manipulated, cheated, insulted, and pressured by circumstances or people. We must let go of negative emotions because they make us prisoners of negative thinking, and therefore, negative results. There is no room for excuses when creating a road map for successful and meaningful living. Practical solutions will be addressed in the chapter of *The Mind*.

Breaking your conditioning is about reaching your truest potential. Many of us are operating on minimum energy levels and don't even know it! If we still cling to conditioned responses (the ones that are problematic), we are busy maintaining other people's ideas of what's right for us. Externally, we may have success in one area of our life, but it doesn't mean that we are operating at our top potential with everything we do. Imagine what you can really achieve if what you desire is fueled by your true potential. Nothing is done halfway. You will release the type of energy that makes anything possible, no matter what it is. Haven't we all heard countless success stories about people changing careers in midlife or later? People are dumping occupations as doctors, trial lawyers and investment bankers, and switching to cooking, landscaping or painting—all for the sake of feeling personally fulfilled and satisfied. What about the success stories of ordinary people fighting for a cause that escalated into something evolutionary nationally, or worldwide? And what about the people who experienced a long and arduous marriage, divorced, and found true love at sixty? Will your choices match your true potential?

THE PROCESS OF BREAKING CONDITIONING

Respect the process of breaking your conditioning. It is a practice that expands over a lifetime and begins with small steps. Express what you want to achieve in your life, and be patient. Always be open to adapting and changing your plan. You are not a failure if you switch course mid-stream. Know that **change is a natural progression toward having the success you desire.**

It can be a scary process because we don't know what to expect, and have to trust that what comes will be good for us. Also, change undoubtedly will involve people we care about, and will induce disagreements and conflict. Sometimes, change will cause us to offend or hurt people who do not understand our choices. Breaking conditioning and embarking on a path of being more of who we are, most likely will present obstacles that we would rather avoid.

What exactly happens when we address our conditioning, and begin to examine what we believe? We step into the unknown, a place filled with situations that are unfamiliar and frightening—even if they are blatantly better, and will lead us toward the life we desire. The troubling thing is that we don't know anything for sure, and our preconditioned response is to run toward what we think is safety—the familiar. Try to resist the pull of what you have been taught is safe, which is the known. The *known* is merely predictable, and the *unknown* is not. Our desire to choose the *known* is an attempt to control things we truly cannot.

Where will the unknown take us? When the process of breaking your conditioning commences, you will feel dramatically better. Many more options exist in the unknown, and although frightening, the unknown does not limit you or your thinking, and thus, does not limit what you can achieve. That feels good. In the unknown, you will begin to get closer to who you really are, and it will become easier to express your true nature. That feels even better. In this process of acquainting yourself with the *real* you, the *new* you will become empowered as an avalanche of choices liberates you from the ball and chain of preconditioned responses. As you engage with new people and undertake new activities, you might be pleasantly surprised by the discovery of new abilities, talents, and skills, originally perceived to be out of reach, or inapplicable, to you.

Breaking conditioning undoubtedly will begin to target your discomfort because you will begin to challenge long-standing beliefs. Be careful of all those around you who continually will reinforce the original conditioning you are trying to change. They are there. How did they get there? In order for us to feel connected with others, we gravitate toward those most like ourselves. Our close friends usually represent a pool of people who agree with us on important issues. They believe what we believe. We like to do the same things, eat the same things, and generally share a lot of common ground. If in your entourage of friends you have those who support you without judgment, cherish them! However, you might want to consider adding new ones who feel the way you do now—and are looking to expand—just like you. **Not all of our relationships can move along with us through cycles of change**. Some relationships do survive the process, but others cannot. It is a good idea to accept and practice the art of *letting go* of the relationships that no longer contribute positively. Those are the relationships that drag you down, and/or away from your true desires. As we all know, relationships can be negative, and can waste precious energy that better could be served in the advancement of who we really are and what we want to become. New friends can make the process of breaking your conditioning easier because they are automatically more supportive. They do not judge the *old* you, and will begin to make you feel comfortable with the *new* you, so the adjustment is less stressful.

The process of breaking your conditioning can be a long one. You'll go back and forth trying to assess why you really have to do any of this. Don't expect immediate results, in fact, don't expect anything but change. And don't be surprised that when you begin to confront conditioning, you begin to experience physical symptoms. Symptoms such as anxiety, panic, and general uneasiness will sneak up to halt the process we so like to avoid, because change is hard. If it were that easy, wouldn't we all be coasting through life without any discomfort?

There's no hurry to do anything. You don't have to know what you want or don't want, nor do you need to know which belief you are ready to challenge. Just practice the following: put yourself into new environments, new situations, and new activities. Make new friends. **The point is to do things that are different and unfamiliar.** You've got a lifetime. New situations will cause you to interact with new people who might inspire you to see life from a different perspective—different from the one you have known. When these moments arise and you are ready to address your conditioning, but only are capable of reflecting on it halfway, step back and come back to it later. You don't want to become a slave to a process that exposes buried emotions. The way conditioning affects us, and why we should continually be aware of its influence, is addressed throughout the chapters of *Body, Mind* and *Spirit.*

Once you address your conditioning, you then can change and become more of the authentic you. You will have the vitality and strength to achieve success at whatever **you** deem important. Bear in mind that you have been programmed and that programming must be undone in order to uncover the best of you. This is the way of the world, and we are all confronted with it, whether consciously or unconsciously. Whether you call it conditioning or change, you are confronted with it. Generally speaking, we are challenged to undo this programming through life events, particularly when crises hit us between the eyes to wake us up!

For example, if we have experienced the controlling behavior of a parent or a spouse, it's only a matter of time before enough resentment piles up to turn into a crisis. Through powerful emotional discomfort, our essence (the real us) forges ahead. This essence of our innate intelligence challenges us to break free from the power structure that has kept us from standing on our own and becoming what we might like to be. Breaking conditioning and escaping the power elements of what we believe takes extraordinary courage. Defying our parents, spouses, friends and other loved ones is always difficult; this is why conditioning has such a stranglehold. It's also why we rationalize, over and over, that what *we want* should be ignored, and why what *they want*, should be implemented. We deny the need for breaking conditioning by assuming *their* choice and insisting that all will work out and won't be so complicated. Think again. Their choice leaves you with no choice, while choosing what you want leaves you with every choice you can imagine. Which sounds better to you?

When making our decisions, there are a few simple rules that we need to integrate. Exercise caution with people, groups, and institutions that claim a monopoly on any one area of expertise, idea, lifestyle, or anything else. This caution also applies to the so-called experts. They too, just like us, are not flawless. Keep in mind that these people are there to give us perspective, broaden and educate us, so that we can make sound decisions and judgments. What we are going to develop is the **intuitive** core that should be accessed, no matter what the choice or decision. It is an amazing resource in our lives, because it correctly guides us when nothing else seems to make any sense.

How do we access this precious resource? This does take concerted effort. As mentioned before, from childhood, we have been conditioned into accepting everyone else's ideas and guidance. It is a difficult process to go against what has been ingrained into our belief system as acceptable. We are so programmed to believe what we believe is right, that when we are confronted with alternative beliefs or ways of doing things, we begin to avoid this internal confrontation. This avoidance is merely the successful shutting down, or putting on hold, our truest potential—and not putting our "true self" into action. **Accessing our life IQ requires deliberate questioning of what we believe, a search for alternatives, and taking action to discover what will work best for us**.

Know that it is not possible to agree with all people whom we encounter during our lifetime. Our personalities are different, as are our likes and dislikes, and we love differently. Not all of us are meant to fall into traditional or conventional patterns. What should we do if convention doesn't agree with how we'd like to do things? Do we continue to follow the norm and relinquish our responsibility to the self? Should we even begin to slide into that notion, the result will be the abdicating of our power to think, act, and fend for ourselves. **THAT** extinguishes any chance for unraveling our true potential. Which way of being will you choose?

Question everything that you read and question all that you are told, unless it sounds "right" to you. That's it. You don't need proof to believe in yourself. Try imposing this way of thinking into all the sources of information around you. Keep in mind that just because someone is an authority doesn't make him or her right. Remember the scandal in the Catholic Church, the scandals at the White House during the presidencies of Richard Nixon and Bill Clinton, the scandal at the

United Nations with the Oil for Food Program, or blatant examples of pernicious leaders like Stalin and Hitler? Use your head and trust your instincts!

Pay close attention to those who want to homogenize society or culture into "it's our way or the highway," who act as though they have figured out what's best for you. These groups can include the majority, but also include any minority groups that shovel their message down your throat. Both groups might be considered as a path for you, but **trust yourself. Get used to asking, "Who said?" and "What makes them right?"** Which identity do you want to uphold? The one that is inherently yours or the one everyone thinks is better for you? Know that when you go against your essence, your internal compass, you are bringing on a lifetime of imbalance.

Try not to separate yourself with categories. For instance, are your friends all the same, interested in what you're interested in, or do you have friends from all walks of life? Is your mind challenged with new thoughts and ideas, as you might be with friends who do different things? Are you afraid of things that are unfamiliar? Do you gravitate toward what you know, what you have been raised with, or what you are told? None of these decisions are undesirable, provided they have been explored. Just try to remember that your individuality cannot be categorized.

When it is our choice, it equals our responsibility. Is that perhaps why we are afraid to do what we want?

Do we allow too many choices to scare us into doing what is easier because we're afraid of making a mistake? Does fear become our comfort zone, indicating when it's time to submit into what is familiar? Careful, everybody. Always question what is conditioning and what is not, to be sure that what you do is entirely *your* decision.

FINDING YOUR ESSENCE

What is your essence? It is who you really are, **your authentic self.** Upon what exactly is your authentic self based on? It's based on having faith in the self—so much faith, that it provides the kind of patience that is steadfast and unrelenting in all pursuits. This faith is the ability to give up control and draw natural confidence in everything that you are. Filtered down, it is what you like and dislike, whom you like and don't like, and toward what you gravitate personally and professionally in absolutely everything you do. Your essence directly is related to your spirit, and it is as individual as your fingerprints.

How do you find your essence? Check your self-esteem, and image (better known as ego). Self-esteem is how you feel about yourself, and ego is whatever face you put forward for people to see. Do they match up? This is extremely important because if your essence is aligned, ALL that relates to you takes an honest approach while representing yourself, both internally and externally. The closer the internal (essence) is with the external (what you represent to others), the more congruent and balanced you are, and the more you project *who* you really are.

Why does this matter? When you are in balance, trusting yourself and others is automatic. The calculation involved in holding up a mask, hiding your true feelings and contorting yourself into the images you think others will approve, becomes completely unnecessary. When you are able to trust, energy is not wasted, but instead is utilized for attaining the success you desire.

When energy is wasted, we become inefficient and stagnant, and operate poorly. It's like a car running on empty, or someone who has chronic low caloric intake. We feel weak and cannot perform as well. The same holds true when we eat too much or absorb high stress levels. Our energy is sluggish and moody, continually operating at low levels. To increase our life IQ, we are looking to operate at our *optimum*, an optimum that encourages equilibrium in all that we might ever do.

Not being who you are, regardless of how you choose to represent yourself, breeds FEAR—fear of showing who you are, fear of not being accepted and not fitting in. You allow convention to rule who you are. The longer you experience insecurity with what society or culture dictates, the more afraid you become of showing and being your true self. Fear prevents our essence from surfacing, thus we fall into the trap of following what everyone else is defining for us. Fear is how we mask our vulnerabilities—something we are desperate to hide.

If you trust who you are, *that* trust is projected forward and others have nothing to accept but what you put forth. Your interaction becomes "This is who I am, take it or leave it." If your intentions are good, it is unlikely that suspicion or second-guessing arises from others, making it impossible to be affected by all the physical pretenses many of us carry into every encounter. There must be balance, and the way to balance the internal with the external, is continually to work on and manage a path of honesty about yourself and your actions. This is the beginning of increasing your life IQ, so let's get started!

III.

BODY

Note: The following information is not meant to be a substitute for medical care and help. If you have serious health issues, seek the advice of trusted medical professionals before undertaking any new regimen.

Increasing your body IQ is about balance, and the following section is a guideline to overall improvement in the health of the body, as well as life extension. A common sense approach involves more than just good habits with eating and exercise. When it comes to your body, your essence plays an important role in determining your health choices. Becoming and being healthy is not as straightforward as it might seem, since it is not only an issue of what you eat and how you exercise, but where you live (the environment), what you do (your work), and where lies your state of mind.

The air you breathe and the water you drink makes a difference. The overall stress levels you absorb, either through the environment, or imposed by you and your relationships, also make a difference in maintaining good health and balance. Stress compromises all that you do, including the body, and "wakes up" your physical weaknesses. Your internal compass is the best solution in determining the cost/benefit of what disciplines you will integrate, and those you will not. Know that all that you do for your body is a choice that is determined by you and you alone.

Keep in mind that it is helpful to make informed choices. Whether you are taking basic steps to change your habits or you feel there is an area that requires more improvement—such as a specific health issue—continued education is critical. It is impossible to learn everything there is to know about taking care of your body, so a proactive approach is recommended. Also, you cannot rely solely on the advice of one doctor or medical professional. Every minute of every day, someone is making new discoveries and implementing new perspectives. If you embrace a flexible attitude with all that you do, including your body and your health, you will continually achieve your optimal balance.

As mentioned before, success results when all three components are in balance.   Balance means equilibrium and overall quality, so you should adhere to **reasonable** choices and solutions when it comes to your body health. Reasonable also refers to the level of effort you impose with each new habit. Too much of anything always will create stress. However, life will present moments of crisis that will tax your body. Hopefully, all that you do will offset any permanent damage that results from those stressful moments. **Radical and extreme solutions should not be undertaken** when selecting these life-changing decisions—unless, of course, you are one of those people who can make extreme changes and stick with them. Most of us cannot.

Let's approach the issue of your body from the beginning. Your body is about maintaining your health, and what you do to keep your life vessel working smoothly. From a scientific point of view, quantum physics has made extraordinary discoveries to validate the human body as being an entire field of energy. This field of energy includes the mental and emotional bodies/planes (also referred to as dimensions). Simply, all are connected, and each has the power to influence the other. Energetic medicine views health and illness as an imbalance of energy flows from all areas of our being. Our field of energy, including that of our mind, emotions and spirit, are made up of countless subatomic particles, which are not solid. However, these particles can combine together to take on material form—and when that happens, it is our physical body. We all have "energy" that manifests from our physical bodies, as well as energy that manifests from our mindset and spirit.

None of us really wants to be sick. Preventing illness should be ever-present in our minds when making decisions to act responsibly with our health choices. This process begins by understanding that there are many body types, and several more distinctions exist between the sexes. Men, for instance, naturally carry less body fat than do women. Some of us have long legs, short waists, or gain and lose weight proportionately, versus those who gain and lose weight in certain areas of their bodies. Some of us naturally carry more muscle mass than others, and the distinctions go on and on. Given that there are many differences in body type, many ways exist to keep your body healthy.

Identify and understand your body type. When you do, you will be better able to access your reserves of energy, and know how energy reserves manifest in your system. In order to get to know your body type, take a good look in the mirror, and don't kid yourself. For instance, if you have large hips, don't think that if you only lost some weight, those hips would disappear. You may lose some inches, but those hips will remain. Get to know your body type and ACCEPT it!

This dilemma of wanting to be something that we are not seems to be the number-one plague infecting the average American. We want to be what society tells us is acceptable, then, society mass-markets how to achieve that impossible goal through thousands of weight loss programs. We are told what and how to eat, and hopefully, we have the body type featured in these programs. Of course, most of us don't, and the entire attempt to mold us into look-a-likes is a well-marketed sham. Also, most of these books completely disregard mental health and the attitudes that should exist in the mind when undertaking change. Rather than approaching good health from a big picture point of view, we fall victim to another long-standing American habit of finding quick-fix solutions to solve our problems.

If you're lanky, hourglass shaped, or built like Hercules, accept it and love it! Take the time to get to know your body. Are you pear-shaped, prone to pile up weight in your hips and thighs, or do you have a figure that gains weight evenly? Do you have a tendency for cellulite, love handles, or a protruding stomach? Are you light on your feet, or heavy-footed when walking? Do you have intensity, or are you a low-keyed personality? They are all interchangeable, and "balance" for anyone can be radically different, which is why a single list for body types—a list that includes distinctions for energy levels and preferences of food that also suits our energy level—does not exist. It's your job to figure it out. Besides making reasonable decisions for our body health, **we will have to take personal responsibility**. Personal responsibility means no whining, no excuses, and particularly, no pointing the finger at others. It is our job to pay attention to what, when, and how we eat, and know that whatever we do, the results are a reflection of our choices alone.

In addition to multiple body types, there are different energy levels amongst people, and these energy levels all express different realities. Have you ever met the type of person we can call "the go, go, go and do, do, do person," who always is on the go, volunteering to do all sorts of chores, and always in the mood to do them?

And if there are ten minutes to spare, he or she will suggest taking on more tasks so as to not waste precious time being unproductive? Then there are people on the opposite end of the spectrum, who haven't a care in the world, aren't concerned if household work hasn't been done, procrastinate, or find "better" things to do. Most of us fall somewhere in the middle. We get our chores done, but we usually don't accomplish them in ten seconds flat.

What **we need to determine,** in addition to our body type, **is the type of energy we are**. How do we do that? Ponder the following: Are you a morning person, full of energy and most alert at that time? Or are you sluggish in the morning, and your best time of day is later in the afternoon? Do you know which one you are, and do you respect those optimal energy periods as the best times to be productive? Whatever you do, don't ever try to keep up with a "go, go, go, and do, do, do," person if your comfort level tells you to do chores spread over time and at a gradual pace. Should you ignore your energy type and try to keep up, you continually will feel tired and won't achieve or accomplish much. Similarly, if your body type is more like a Rubens model, don't expect to look like Angelina Jolie. But should you attempt to defy the reality of your body and energy type, you also will create undue mental and physical stress, defeating your original goal of staying healthy and in shape. You will be out of balance and will not perform optimally. Besides, who said Angelina Jolie, or some other actress or model type, is better, anyway? Always separate what is, and is not conditioning. Be positive about your body type and image, and realistic about your energy level, as this will promote natural confidence and optimism.

Our mind and body type have innate tendencies, and every event in our mind equates to our body and vice versa. So imagine, if you are chronically caught up with thoughts of looking like a model—or down on yourself for not having a more voluptuous (female) or muscular (male) physique, while your body type is completely the opposite—you will expend negative energy. That energy would be better utilized improving the things that are improvable, which invariably creates positive energy and natural confidence. Do you want stress or do you wish to feel and look better? Know that the body and the mind are inextricably linked, and the two rely on each other to maintain balance. So don't think that you can fool your body into becoming model-like or Hercules when it cannot. That's the reason radical diets do not work—they only create temporary results that appease our nagging desire for instantaneous success.

Additionally, know that our body functions are purposeful, not a haphazard collection of matter just going along and doing something. We need to take care of those functions. However, our bodies are amazingly resilient and can tolerate a great deal of abuse, which explains why we can escape physical breakdown and serious illness for a long time. So, watch out, those of you who are forty or younger, thinking you're invincible and arrogantly practicing bad habits. They will catch up with you when you least expect!

Ponder the following: Why do you think there are mandatory tests and procedures once you're over forty or fifty, like a colonoscopy, cholesterol, bone-density, and other tests to determine good health? Those tests are meant to check on what damage you have incurred—and most of us have. The medical community is quite confident that something eventually will show up. How do you think they determined the average age for those tests? They are aware that on average, our forties and fifties are the times when chronic problems become physically apparent. However, some of us no longer have to wait until we are forty or fifty. Sadly, there are multiple statistics that cite a tremendously high percentage of childhood obesity, which inevitably leads to heart problems and diabetes at earlier and earlier ages. **We don't die of old age, but of a breakdown of our system**. A strong life IQ defies the notion that age determines illness, and instead, suggests that preventive steps can be taken for life extension. Our choices for a healthier lifestyle should not be postponed. They should become a priority that strongly will determine the quality of our health throughout our lifetime.

According to the CDC (Centers for Disease Control and Prevention website page/Chronic Disease Prevention and Health Promotion), chronic diseases such as cancer, heart ailments and diabetes are the leading causes of death and disability in the United

States. Many experts agree that these chronic illnesses could be avoided by integrating healthier lifestyles. This is the goal for increasing your life IQ.

Let's delve deeper into some scientific explanations of how a healthier lifestyle prevents chronic illnesses. Back in high school biology, we learned that every cell in our body goes through the process of mitosis. It is one cell dividing perfectly into another, and another, and another. This is how we live and grow. It then stands to reason that if our cells do not function properly because of poor health choices and an inability to decrease stress, some cells will not divide properly. Cancer is one of the risks when our cells malfunction and mutate.

Remember high school chemistry and the litmus test? We were given small rectangular strips of paper that determined whether pH levels were more acid or more alkaline. Why does this matter? Our body chemistry also requires certain pH levels, and the type of food we eat and stress levels we endure, modify those pH levels to either healthy or unhealthy levels. Prolonged, unhealthy pH levels cause chronic illnesses. The problem is that most of us don't pay attention to pH levels. By the time our pH level is dangerously unhealthy, an illness has occurred. Further, we accept the illness we have incurred, get medicated, and do little to change our habits. Why is that? It's easier to take medications to suppress our symptoms, rather than take greater responsibility for our entire health. **A holistic approach is needed in order to maintain**

balance, and offset the risks of chronic illness. It is not helpful that our society generally encourages simplistic thinking—that each symptom and ailment can be alleviated by an appropriate medication. So, rather than just alleviating symptoms, we should focus on discovering the root of how the illness or problem originated.

ENERGY LEVELS

Take the time to understand what works best for you. For instance, eating breakfast might not be as necessary for you as for someone who is more active or rises earlier than you do. Perhaps you're not the sort who wakes up super alert, but instead, are groggy and slow-moving. **Not every body digests food identically, and not all foods react in a body the same way**. For instance, starches are broken down into sugars, but a person's activity level determines how it is stored or utilized. If you aren't terribly active, but eat an inordinate amount of starches (potatoes, pasta, breads), particularly at night, it will be stored rather than utilized, and you will gain weight. Also, some of us need more protein in our diet, and others need more carbohydrates. Can you recognize which one you are? Have you ever paid attention, particularly when energy levels wane? Did you know that the intake of food groups varies, depending on your age and activity level? **Start practicing the art of paying attention to your body and energy levels,** in order to make the appropriate choices for *you*. No one but *you* can make that determination.

Ask the question: How do I feel soon after I eat any food, and are there symptoms of discomfort or fatigue? If so, do I ignore them, or take a pill, and continue to eat what my body is telling me is not right for me? This is the beginning of discovering what foods are right for you. It is also the moment you begin to *trust* your body.

Ask the question: If I discovered that I had allergic reactions to food, such as lactose intolerance, would I stop eating dairy, but still consume diet sodas and fast foods filled with cancer causing chemicals, or hydrogenated fats that promote considerable health risks? Do I respect one aspect of my health, while consuming other foods that are truly more harmful in the long-run?

Ask the question: When I put on weight, what foods were responsible for that weight gain? Be responsible and figure that out.

Do you ever notice the type of people who spend hours in the gym, frantic about keeping up with the body type they just don't have? Are you acquainted with people who keep going on the latest diet, and who are spiraling up and down in weight? Are you aware that those people have developed neurotic and compulsive behavior, are putting stress on their organs, and might later develop chronic health problems, just to keep up with something that inevitably will fail? Like us all, you too, may have fallen into this unadvertised trap of becoming health conscious. Think about it. What do you do when you have exercised strenuously for, let's say a half an hour and a joint begins to hurt? Do you press on because you told yourself (or the book you read told you) your routine MUST last an hour, or it won't serve its purpose? Do you stop and not push that joint into potential injury? Stressing body parts is what happens to some athletes. In the spirit of competition, they push and stress their abilities past normal limits to win, regardless of pain. Inevitably, these athletes face surgery and physical breakdown before their time. Winning may be the only pursuit that makes them feel alive and happy, but most of us simply don't fall into that category. Understand that too much exercise can be harmful, as well. We all have a barometer that tells us exactly what we need, but unless we practice good habits, that barometer isn't working.

If we all had time to spend on reading and educating ourselves on all aspects of health, exercise, and food, two things undoubtedly would come up. First, you would notice that there are many ways to keep your body healthy. Second, if you wanted positive results, you would have to change your habits permanently. Common sense tells us that you alone can determine if a small or large breakfast makes the most sense, and if fresh juice or salmon works best for you. Also, the exercise you choose to undertake—vigorous or light, every day or three times a week—will be entirely up to you. Countless experts have opinions on exercise, and how and what to eat. To assess the efficacy of such advice, take a look around. Have you ever seen so many overweight people in your life? If experts all purport to know the *best* way to achieve this backbreaking chore to good health, and we live in a period where information is abundant, why are Americans becoming unhealthier by the minute? Always question what is conditioning—and what is best for you.

Let's be clear. We need to continue to educate ourselves about the body, and to appreciate many of the sources of information on nutrition, exercise, and health. It's beneficial to read all that we can. However, many, if not all of us, have been overwhelmed with the many choices, left confused about what is right for us. A book of all solutions does not exist, which is why you need to respect what your body *tells* you. Additionally, we haven't the time to completely and thoroughly investigate all that is right for us. That's part of the challenge. The bottom line is: **Staying healthy is a lifelong commitment**.

Getting to know and learning to take care of your body cannot be accomplished in a few months, as some might want you to believe. It is a commitment to add, subtract, and change regimens as life goes on. You cannot discover overnight what foods work best for you. There are too many foods. You also will not discover the most efficient type of exercise by just reading a book or following the latest craze. That's why hundreds of books, exercise regimens and machines exist to show you how to stay healthy. It is important to read as many books and experiment as much as possible to determine what feels right to you. Over time, you will begin to notice an overlapping of suggestions and advice that jumps off the page because it particularly suits YOU. Give it a try, and see if you are comfortable. If not, abandon that discipline. Take your time in beginning each regimen, and don't pressure yourself with unrealistic expectations. Anything worthwhile doesn't come overnight, so in addition to practicing the art of paying attention to our body and energy levels, **practice the art of patience** when it comes to your health.

Eating and exercise boil down to balance, and it's never too late to start. Each and every discipline you integrate will slowly but surely wake up that barometer that will indicate what is comfortable for you. Don't get overwhelmed by tackling everything at once. Moderation is a good word to impose on these choices, but remember that the scale varies for everyone. Light exercise might be all that you need to boost your energy just enough to sustain positive energy levels, whereas adding another fifteen minutes because you're wrestling to be five pounds lighter, will cause a drop in your best energy level. Your body always will respond positively when you find the correct foods and correct exercise. Pay attention to all physical symptoms, and do what's right for you. **Trust your body signals**.

Moderation in eating and exercise is the best way to discover what agrees and disagrees with your body. Make your body your best friend by making sure that all you do for it is done out of love and respect, and not some exasperating goal of perfection that in the real world will add up to nothing more than temporary euphoria and guaranteed failure, let alone health problems. You might say, "Well, I am happier looking super-thin," or, "I need to body-build so the women will swoon over me." Fine—go right ahead. How long do you think you will maintain that false reality? Do you believe vapid images will sustain or contribute positively to your golden years? Are you planning to keel over before you see a line on your face? When it comes to our body, we all have to think a little bit more long-term, as experts are projecting average life spans to increase to one hundred and twenty years, provided, of course, that we take care of our health. Other experts have projected life spans to increase to one hundred and fifty years! Will you look at the bigger picture when it comes to your body decisions? Will you promote enough quality and balance to satisfy good health into old age?

If you drop to a weight that is unhealthy for your body type, over time, subtle changes will occur internally. What is that unhealthy weight? It is a weight that you cannot maintain without being uncomfortable and fatigued, or becoming a slave to dieting and its restrictions. It is a weight you force upon yourself by erratic eating patterns, missed meals, and inconsistencies. Eating erratically and inconsistently stresses the body and its organs—inviting inflammation, illness and disease. Although superficially thinner, the damage you are causing will be internal and not readily apparent, thus masking the insidious nature of your weight loss result. Just keep in mind, that one day, the extreme choice of being super-thin or looking like Hercules will take its toll on your body, and you might wake up with a debilitating disease or diseases. All of us are terribly aware of the rampant eating disorders, such as anorexia and bulimia, and for the muscle building types, steroid use. None of that has healthy results. If we delve deeper into these disorders surrounding our "image," such investigation would reveal poor self-concepts, which really stem from problems in the mind.

We must then reflect: While we are young and shortsighted, is our body image so important that later, it will turn us into older, useless people with chronic aches and pains, or premature death? Are you one of those people who think that this cannot happen to you? Thinking this way also is a choice, and it is yours to make. However, you also can choose to be less extreme and genuinely interested in making body health improvements for a lifetime.

Your life IQ for the body will increase by adhering to three simple disciplines and practicing five basic steps for good eating. Whether choosing what to eat or how to exercise, common sense requires the following:

1. Practice moderation.
2. Pay attention to your body type and energy level, and make lifelong changes where appropriate.

3. Be realistic, practice patience, and eliminate the *pressure* of expecting instantaneous results.

What's Good to Eat

You've heard it a hundred times before. Eat a low-fat, nutrient-dense diet. Eat leafy vegetables, fruit, less sugar, and less fat. Drink green tea and other exotic teas from Asia that contain antioxidants and have healing properties, and in some cases, are cancer-fighting beverages. Decrease your intake of red meat, and choose fish and poultry. Eat super foods (there are too many to list, but these foods are nutrient dense), as well as raw foods. Raw foods retain the highest levels of nutrients and enzymes. Note that if you eat raw foods, be sure it is organic all the way! Eliminate smoking, and cut down on alcohol, soda, and caffeine. If you do any, stock up on antioxidants. Alcohol, smoking, caffeine, and stress, deplete your antioxidant reserves, leaving you in the red, putting you out of balance and at risk for disease. Know that second-hand smoke can be just as harmful as smoking. Avoid fast and processed foods, (all empty calories, and low nutritional value), artificial sweeteners, and trans-fatty oils.

Consider taking supplements, particularly a probiotic (this will be addressed in the section of Supplements on p. 71). Switch from iodized salt to sea salt, which is unprocessed. Drink only purified or filtered water, preferably at room temperature, at least sixty-four ounces a day. Teas, fruit juices, milk, and other drinks do not count and should NOT be substituted for water. Water naturally washes away toxins, and the closer to room temperature it is, the easier it is on your digestion—a bodily function that *must* be respected and is addressed shortly.

OK, those two paragraphs were dense with information, but it is the bottom line to good health. Feel free to add or subtract any suggestions, as well as purchasing any book or books that write about good things to eat. You do not have to adhere to everything that is said or written. Gravitate to the type of eating and foods you think you can maintain in a healthy diet. Along the same thinking, consider eating for your blood type. *Eat Right 4 Your Blood Type: The Individualized Diet Solution to Staying Healthy, Living Longer & Achieving Your Ideal...*by Peter J. DAdamo and Catherine Whitney, is a fascinating book that reveals what foods work better in your system and according to your blood type. Depending on your blood type, certain foods metabolize better, while others do not. Some of us are natural born meat eaters, while others should become vegetarians.

When it comes to healthy eating, consider doing one step at a time. For instance, try to cut down on animal fat and substitute with healthy unsaturated fats like those found in nuts and olive oil, slowly, and over time. And that's it. Do that until you've mastered a change in fat intake, and it's no longer an effort. Then take another step, like slowly increasing fruits and vegetables into your diet. Add or subtract as many foods as you like, but don't overdo it. Too much change generally leads to becoming overwhelmed. It will be difficult at first, because you will have to focus more on what you are eating, which is why you don't want to do too much, too soon. The goal is to integrate foods and discipline you're ready to incorporate for a lifetime. Do not vacillate with that commitment. As soon as you slack off a little here, a little there, the entire effort will soon disappear.

If you cannot make a lifetime commitment, don't bother! Temporary successes will only lead to feelings of discouragement and possible depression when you failed, and the gaps between success and failure gradually will widen. You will feel worse than when you originally started. However, don't beat yourself up if this happens to you a few times. Remember that you always have another chance. That is why it is important to take on disciplines a little at a time. Small successes are better than none at all. Over time, your healthier choices will become second nature, rather than an arduous effort and a chore.

In the spirit of success, we all should appreciate the people who can admit that they are unable to maintain the best of health habits, or that they don't want to. The result of these choices leaves them, at least, with a better state of mind. For our goal, it is either healthy—or it is not. You are choosing either one or the other. Staying healthy is non-negotiable. Treat your diet like going to school. We mostly begin in kindergarten and cannot expect to do Calculus before tackling simple adding and subtracting. Take one step at a time, and if you have to repeat a grade, so be it.

There is common sense when it comes to healthy eating. Don't force yourself to eat anything that you don't like, but do try new, healthy things to eat. Also, you will have to change your eating habits—everything from how much you eat, and when. If you don't like something that is healthy, don't eat it. Find an alternative, if one exists. Let's say that you detest kale, which is probably one of the healthiest leafy vegetables to eat. However, you are not doomed when it comes to staying healthy. Simply, do not eat it, and move on to something else. Perhaps you don't like soy products. Nothing is mandatory, except that you choose healthy foods. Chances are that you have enough to do, so bypass that food item, and make an effort elsewhere. Spending too much time fussing about food items detracts from the basic purpose of staying healthy. We don't need extra reasons to give up. **Start adding healthy foods and subtracting unhealthy foods** a little at a time; it glosses over that feeling of becoming overwhelmed. How much should one eat of that healthy food? Eat enough to feel satisfied; any more will compromise your digestion.

When should one eat? Only you know the best times. First, eat when you are hungry. Don't postpone a meal because you think it isn't quite the time to eat. For instance, it is 11:30 AM and you planned on having lunch at one. Although hungry, you postpone eating until one o'clock. The only thing that you achieve, particularly when first integrating better eating habits, is an insatiable hunger that will cause you to overeat, thus eating more than you originally planned. Also, it is likely that you will eat too quickly and invite poor digestion. Self-control is harder to impose on starving animals, which is what we turn into when changing our dietary habits. We feel deprived and quickly compensate by eating larger portions. Consider making dinner the lightest meal of the day. Evening is the moment we all slow down, so most of the calories from dinner will go unused and eventually will be stored as fat. Additionally, it is a good idea to limit the intake of desserts prior to 3 PM. They will burn off by the time we go to bed.

Changing Your Eating Habits

This is not a diet book, so there will not be specific recommendations for your meals. However, we will make some suggestions that will contribute to healthy living by adding quality and maintaining balance. You want to make some intelligent decisions along with assessing a reasonable cost/benefit to everything you do. In other words, if you choose to eat desserts, know that the benefit of this food will cost you—in terms of a little more exercise, or an extra pound added to your weight. So, if you're a busy person trying to lose weight, and have barely enough time to finish all your work, bypass dessert because you won't have the time for exercise!

DIGESTION

We need to be concerned about our digestion because it is an integral part of staying healthy. Digestion is how we metabolize our food and air intake. Air and food break down into molecules that convert into energy. Understandably, the quality of your air and food contributes to how well and efficiently those molecules are broken down—that energy either is used or stored. If digestion is incomplete, so is its ability to take advantage of optimal energy and its use. It than would make sense that our body can malfunction, begin to compensate, and deplete its overall efficiency. Give or take, that's what we are talking about when it comes to good digestion. Digestion is very important because with inefficient energy or fuel, or none whatsoever, we malfunction, or don't function at all. Ultimately, this situation sounds like premature death, but not before we contract so many diseases and illnesses that we exist in a living hell. How well we digest also is connected to how well our immune system functions. Know that seventy per cent (70%) of the immune system is associated with the colon (see Probiotics p. 73).

Bad foods and a lack of exercise contribute to incomplete digestion, thus, contributing to imbalances. When imbalanced, rather than feeling good with lots of energy, you have inertia and feel sluggish. Processed and fast foods will slow you down; they are difficult to digest. Fresher and less processed food is easier to digest. Is it a wonder that so many Americans suffer with indigestion, eating on the go, and excusing that a meal should bear the sacrifice in their busy schedule? Think again. If you truly are on the go, then you especially need to think about what you're eating. Bad moods ensue with bad foods, and all of that goes straight to the office where you need to perform at your best. It is wise to eat slowly and in peace. Be respectful that your body is performing a major task. Try making lunch your main meal. It is old time wisdom that helps you burn what you've eaten throughout the day. *If* you must eat desserts, lunch is the best time. The guilt and calories will wear off by the day's end.

Don't stuff yourself regularly like people do at Thanksgiving. Eating past the point of satisfaction also encourages incomplete digestion. Even healthy foods cause balance or imbalance, depending on body type. This is why you must respect what your body tells you. If a food item makes you feel lousy, slow, or sick, gives you stomach pain or too much gas—don't eat it! There's nothing else to debate. For example, some of us adore the flavoring of onions or garlic to food, and we recognize their health benefits. However, some of us experience major intestinal discomfort, which is a clear signal to eat smaller amounts or eliminate those foods completely. If spicy foods agree with you, eat all that you want. Why put your body through painful disruption for the sake of the well-documented problems of acid reflux, ulcers, and other GI tract diseases? This principle of using physical discomfort as a gauge for what to eat also holds true for foods that are healthy, but not for you. Don't eat them! Happily, we live in a country with an abundance and variety of foods. So, when food irritates or aggravates your body in any way, don't worry about the rules; trust your internal signals to direct you.

Try to adhere to consistent eating times. This programs your body to expect the same time to digest and refuel; it respects the process. Get to know your energy cycles. Are you more energetic early in the morning, or later in the day? Gauge your mealtimes around what your body tells you are the best times to fuel up for energy. Just be consistent. Bear in mind that if you're eating organic and on the go, exercising at night, and not getting enough sleep, bad digestion will offset anything positive that you are doing. If you change one thing, change this: **Better digestion = better energy.** Alive versus sluggish—you decide.

There are five steps for marked body health improvement:

1. Eat as fresh as possible.
2. Take supplements.
3. Drink water, and lots of it!
4. Get enough sleep
5. Do moderate exercise.

If you do anything first, get started by eating foods as fresh as possible. These are foods that have little or no processing. That means eat foods that have had little done to them before you purchase them. For instance, if you buy a vegetable, buy it fresh, not packaged and cooked, or with additives or preservatives. If you buy ice cream, make sure ALL of the ingredients are those you understand. Simply, try to eat unprocessed foods that you like. Remember, cooking is a process, and few of us actually can eliminate cooking and only eat raw foods. But if you can eat some raw foods, like fruit and vegetables, it is a fabulous compliment to eating healthy. By eating raw, you will absorb the highest amount of natural nutrients. Should you be unable to avoid sweets, be sure they are natural and unprocessed—like those available in a bakery. Avoid processed cakes, cookies, and candy bars—which brings us to the next step in assuring better health.

Eating fresh automatically will eliminate all partially hydrogenated oils and artificial sweeteners. They are cancer causing when breaking down in our bodies. Partially hydrogenated oils are found in many baked goods, cookies, chips, and candy bars. One reason those oils and sweeteners exist is because they are cheaper to manufacture, and have a deceptively addicting taste that fools us into its consumption. Also, the reason that they are unhealthy is because our bodies do not recognize artificial anything. Our body immediately rejects what is not organic and begins to compensate in order to metabolize these ingredients. Over time, these ingredients tax our system in a way where chronic problems occur. This will be addressed in more detail in the section of Toxins. However, it is important to note that finally, the U.S. Food and Drug Administration (FDA) took a step toward banning trans fats. In November 2013, the agency announced its preliminary finding that partially hydrogenated oils (PHOs) – trans fat - are not "generally recognized as safe" for use in food.

If you want to eat bread and sweets, go to a bakery and inquire if they use these unhealthy oils. Generally speaking, they do not, but you still need to ask. As for candy and chocolate, go to specialized garden markets, where they carry American or European brands that generally avoid these poisoning ingredients. Pay particular attention to artificial sweeteners—those pink, blue or yellow packets found in the bowl next to the sugar, or are added to diet sodas and other diet foods. There is countless data on aspartame and artificial sweeteners and their harmful effects on the body, and we would highly recommend your further investigation.

Avoiding sweets always is best, but it isn't terribly realistic with most of us. Always choose sweets with natural ingredients including sugar, (unrefined is best, but if refined or unrefined, make sure it is labeled cane sugar), over chemical concoctions containing harmful sugar substitutes, additives, colorings, and preservatives. If you have to eat sweets, make sure you can understand the ingredients. There are many options these days, but **you must become accustomed to reading all labels**, and to ask when labels aren't available. If you eat fresh food, eating fast and processed foods will be out of the question.

It can seem drastic and difficult to eat fresh, but it is a habit like any other. Know that your body possesses a subtle meter that tells you what it wants to eat. However, if you have been one to eat badly, this instrument is rusty and tends to malfunction. You now believe that fast, processed food, sugar, and salt are the only things worth eating. You will have to be patient in overcoming these addictive taste patterns. As said before, try one thing at a time, but it is important to stress the elimination of processed and fast foods because of their preservatives, additives, and partially hydrogenated oils that alter your natural chemistry. Besides filling ourselves with chemicals and empty calories, we will be setting ourselves up for chronic illness and disease. We cannot attain good health, let alone feel well and be full of energy, on pseudo non-organic foods.

There is no rush when it comes to common sense. If you start by eating healthier and fresher foods, you still get to eat what you have been eating—such as a hamburger and French fries. Just make it a hamburger with no hormones or antibiotics, and French fries cooked with no hydrogenated oils. Of course, if you want to lose weight, don't expect to if you don't pay attention to fat intake. Use your head. Eating fresh will be easier on your digestion because of the natural and organic state of fresh food. The end result will be the successful distribution of all those nutrients to the right places in your body, thus improving your energy level. You might even lose weight because all was metabolized properly. Vitamins, minerals, and enzymes decrease with each level of processing, so watch out for those pre-packaged, readymade frozen dinners that claim to be healthy, but deliver mostly empty calories.

Do you ever wonder how additives and chemicals entered the scene as being safe for our digestion and our health? They're not. Additives and chemicals cleverly have been inserted by claims of being in such small doses that they aren't harmful. How did that happen? And why aren't more of us paying more attention to statistics citing the dangers of preservatives, artificial sweeteners, and trans-fats? Sadly, we, the consumers, are the ones responsible. Admittedly, this process did begin with the intention of making food cheaper to manufacture and to last longer, but mainly, manufacturers follow the great American demand of "fast and easy." We seem to be more interested in satisfying our time constraints, instead of our health. It then would follow that the misplaced priority of fast and easy, along with those unattainable images that society has put forth as acceptable, skews our responsibility away from health.

We're all supposed to be super-thin, super-fast, and super-rich. So, rather than taking a sound approach to staying healthy by maintaining healthy weight levels, and stressing preventive health from childhood, we have been programmed into a belief that is counterintuitive. We think that we should lose that weight as fast as possible, become what we cannot, take drugs to mask symptoms of these bad choices, and pump ourselves full of chemicals to achieve the unachievable. Does that exhaustive process make any sense? If vitamins, minerals, and enzymes decrease with each level of processing, wouldn't it also make sense that eating a pre-packaged frozen dinner is useless, and in fact, unhealthy? Again, it all is a matter of choice. However, the more bad stuff you eliminate from your diet, the more you can help yourself when illness does strike. When healthy, your body will be in better condition to deal with that illness. **The fact that you can stumble along on empty calories, and pop drugs to suppress symptoms that will inevitably lead to more serious illnesses, should not be acceptable**.

Start off by eating what you have been, but as fresh as possible. That will automatically eliminate the bad stuff we just mentioned. Wouldn't it be better to eat pastries with the best of ingredients, rather than one that is a processed, full of additives and preservatives of a frozen dinner? You see, a new healthy pattern doesn't mean that we only will eat pastries. It really translates into a choice of not eating dangerous chemicals, preservatives, or fats in any amount—period. We can walk off the extra pounds, but can we reverse the damage brought on by the chemicals that eventually alter our DNA?

To review our goal: Start paying attention to body type and energy levels, and begin by eating fresh. When you've undertaken eating as fresh as possible, try eating new foods, and avoid any that cause adverse reactions.

SUPPLEMENTS

Ponder the following when considering the use of supplements. Our environment is no longer what it used to be. Where we live, whether in a city, suburb, or rural area, determines how polluted our environment is, including the air we breathe and the water we drink. The choices we make in our food will determine how much nutrition we actually are consuming. Even if we eat healthy and organically, there will be times when unbeknownst toxins such as GMOs (genetically modified organism), antibiotics, or hormones may be present in our food. Our lifestyle, job, and everyday life will determine how much stress we are absorbing. All of these modern-day challenges lead to nutritional deficiencies. The reason we all need to consider taking supplements is because those pollutants, toxins and stress levels deplete our system's daily reserves. In other words, we don't have enough to satisfy our usual daily levels, let alone enough nutrients to combat those pollutants, toxins and stress levels. We are left with a chronic shortage of nutrients, operating on "not enough." The longer we continue on "not enough," the more susceptible we are to illness and disease.

What supplements should we take? Without a doubt, our first choice should be a probiotic. (For those suffering with chronic digestive issues, consider taking digestive enzymes in addition to probiotics). Probiotics do more than just help with digestion. They boost your immune system by making sure the flora in your gut is functioning properly. Enhanced immunity means you can experience fewer colds and flus, combat allergies and increase your energy. Probiotics can reverse ulcers, irritable bowel syndrome, and many other gut inflammatory diseases because probiotics make sure that your gut has all of the *right* bacteria to perform its function. Also, a healthy gut flora balance helps prevent cancer and radiation damage from X-rays and CT scans. "Probiotics have a promising future in the prevention of several cancers. The most promising evidence is [regarding] colon cancer. Probiotic intervention has been shown in studies to bind and deactivate carcinogens. They promote immune function, inhibit carcinogen-producing enzymes, and influence the overgrowth of flora in the gut. Since nearly 70% of the immune system is associated with the colon, a probiotic immune boosting influence provides protection against harmful viral and bacterial strains and promotes tumor inhibition". (The Probiotic Cancer Relationship Source: Cancer-General • Author: Vanessa Wada, MS, RD)

Another reason you may consider taking a probiotic is if you have been eating the typical American diet of processed foods that includes too much fat, sugar and salt. This type of diet interferes with proper digestion, and over time, the function of your colon diminishes. GMOs are used in many processed foods. Antibiotics and hormones are present in non-organic meat, dairy products and farm raised fish. These ingredients destroy probiotic bacteria, and therefore, we need to take a probiotic to replace the good bacteria that is lost. Do your research. Unless you take the time to investigate, rebuking this information is easy.

So much is being discovered regarding the benefits of probiotics, but consider the following as a measure of how probiotics may actually help with your overall health. Dr. Natasha Campbell-McBride, a United Kingdom neurologist, cured her son of autism. She created a diet that restored his probiotic levels into balance and helped heal his inflammatory conditions. This diet, GAPS (Gut and Psychology Syndrome), confirmed the connection with gut health and mental health. She has a full-time practice and treats children and adults with autism, learning disabilities, neurological disorders, psychiatric disorders, immune disorders and digestive problems. She discovered that children are particularly prone to vaccine damage, and the GAPS nutritional program is an effective treatment for autism, ADHD, dyslexia, dyspraxia, depression, and schizophrenia. Her book, *Gut and Psychology Syndrome: Natural Treatment for Autism, Dyspraxia, ADD, Dyslexia, ADHD...Depression* is an excellent read.

How to Choose a Probiotic

Look for powdered probiotics or probiotic capsules that are filled with powder. These are the most effective form of probiotics. Liquid probiotics are not as effective and do not have a long shelf life. Pick a probiotic that has at least 1 billion organisms per gram. Anything less won't be a big benefit to your body's health. Look for a variety of strains, and choose one with at least eight different strains. Choose probiotics that are not centrifuged. This means that the manufacturer did not use centrifuging as its processing method. The centrifuging process makes the living organisms in probiotics useless. Check the label, and if it's not written, move on to another brand.

Multi-Vitamins & Multi-Minerals

The second supplement we should consider taking is a multi-vitamin and multi-mineral formula. Which one do we choose? If you currently are taking a multi-vitamin and multi-mineral supplement, do you know what type of supplement you have selected? Just like any product that we may buy, there are differences in the quality and manufacturing, including that of vitamins and minerals. Supplements are manufactured as synthetic, semi-synthetic, or whole food. Synthetic are not natural—they are human made in a laboratory. Semi-synthetic are a combination of human made and natural, and whole food is completely natural. Whole food supplements also can be distinguished by their higher quality—and those supplements are labeled organic. Learning how to read a label is critical to understanding what you are actually buying. And if you do not understand what is on the label, look it up. It isn't until you begin to look things up, that you begin to learn how supplements are distinguished and why some are dangerous.

The difference between whole food supplements and synthetic supplements is this: whole food supplements are made from concentrated whole food, and are recognized by the body to fully support your body and immune system. Nature intended that we consume whole foods because all of the vitamins, minerals, antioxidants, enzymes, coenzymes, trace elements, activators and many other unknown or undiscovered factors **are found together**. Their structure is highly complex and they are found in the correct synergy. Therefore, whole foods deliver the right combination of nutrients into your body and are properly absorbed. Delivered in any other way, nutrition is compromised. The label of a whole food supplement will display the ingredients by sourcing from what fruits or vegetables it was derived, and if it is organic.

Synthetic supplements contain isolated and fragmented nutrients. That means that each nutrient is only a part of the whole. Synthetic supplements are made in a laboratory, and although the isolated nutrients have an identical chemical structure as the whole food derived nutrition, they do not deliver the same results. Synthetic supplements cannot be expected to do the same job as a whole food when it is only one, isolated part of that whole food. By only being a part of the whole, the benefit is compromised. This means that you are not receiving the full benefit that nature intended. Further, these isolated nutrients are manufactured with potentially toxic solvents and other chemicals. If you read the label, you will see the list of the isolated vitamins and minerals (they will not be sourced as being from fruits and vegetables), but then, there will be other ingredients (such as phosphate, magnesium stearate, and magnesium chloride, all of which are chemicals).

Just like refined foods, synthetic supplements can create numerous problems and imbalances in your body if taken at high levels for long periods of time. When we consume supplements that contain isolated vitamins, sometimes we are getting too much of one vitamin and not enough of the other. This imbalance can be very dangerous and cause health problems. Synthetic supplements can act more like drugs in your body, forcing themselves down one pathway or another. Due to the lack of absorption, these supplements can stress the liver and kidneys, as the body tries to detoxify and eliminate the excess. It is better to rely on high quality food and whole food supplements to ensure proper absorption.

Semi-synthetic are a combination of synthetic and natural ingredients, and they may contain herbal ingredients. You will notice that if they are natural, they will list the source of that herb or plant from which they were derived. Remember to check if the vitamins and/or minerals have whole food sources. These are the basics for supplementation, but more can be added, depending on health issues and recommendations by your medical professional—preferably one who is educated in nutrition and holistic medicine. When you are buying supplements, consider going to health food stores only. They are filled with knowledgeable people who can answer many questions. Finally, consider supplementing with extra

Vitamin C and other antioxidant formulas that help boost your immune system, particularly during colder weather, higher than normal stress levels, or any other periods that might compromise your optimal energy level.

A word of advice: Understand that no supplement alone will help you achieve the level of health you desire. You will have to make lifestyle and behavior changes, while also taking supplements to achieve ultimate physical health.

WATER

Drink plenty of water. Room temperature is best for digestion. Colder temperatures cause your digestion to work harder. Either way, just make sure it's purified or filtered. It is a natural cleanser of your system, and it flushes out toxins. If you don't drink enough water, you may experience frequent colds and toxins may collect in your system. Over time, you will increase your risk for illness. A lack of water also contributes to dry and prematurely aged skin, but more importantly, chronic dehydration compromises the proper functioning of cells, again, providing fertile ground for the onset of illness. For the many health benefits of water, consider reading the following book: *Your body's many cries for water: You are not sick, you are thirsty,* by F. Batmabghelidj.

TOXINS

Admitted to or not, most of us live in a toxic

environment. It's the nature of living on earth these days. Some of us live in an environment worse than others. We tolerate sensory assaults in cities, pollutants in the water we drink and the air we breathe. Environmental pollutants such as radiation, cigarette smoke, and herbicides can spawn free radicals, which further can compromise our health. It's unrealistic to eliminate it all, but every discipline we take to improve our health adds to our overall quality of life. That's why, despite the difficulty, it's worth the effort to change to fresher eating habits, take appropriate and quality supplements, and drink purified or filtered water no matter where we are—to protect our body health.

Toxins enter our system through the air we breathe, the water we drink, the food we eat, and the products we put on our skin. If we ignore the need to eliminate toxins, over time, these small, seemingly acceptable amount of poisons can build up in our system and cause significant health issues. We need to question the safety of any toxin. So-called "safe" levels of anything, including radiation, should be investigated. Since we already have determined that everything about our bodies is different, don't you think that differences exist in the amount of radiation, chemicals or safe levels of any toxin we individually can tolerate? The truth is that those organizations who determine "safe" levels cannot specifically say what is safe for everybody. However, they are sure to inform us that pregnant women and weaker individuals who have compromised immune systems are forbidden to have x-rays. Obviously, if you are in an accident and need to be x-rayed, you get x-rayed because it determines your injuries. However, precautionary x-raying, such as at the dentist or doctor, may be unwise. You or I may be the unlucky ones who will not tolerate any added levels of radiation. Our health habits and where we live also will determine our ability to absorb radiation before we contract illness or disease. Does anyone really know acceptable levels of toxins? What would compel us to accept a standard for upsetting our body equilibrium via harmful, foreign substances? We have enough to do to avoid illness of any kind, so why should we absorb more toxins when we know there is a connection to illness? **YOUR LIFE IQ encourages research so that you can make informed decisions regarding toxins.**

SLEEP

Get to know your true sleep cycle, not the cycle you have imposed upon your life. Sleep deprivation and the excuses we have for not sleeping adequately, adds stress to the body. Over the long term, that stress level will undermine your body and its health. If sleep is something you choose to disrespect, it is your choice. Remember, saying "I can't" is a choice. If health becomes important in any way, it will become impossible to ignore your body's need for proper sleep and rejuvenation.

On the side of vanity, sleep is one of the biggest factors in maintaining an excellent appearance, and perhaps through some personal pride, you might consider more sleep. Well-rested people don't look worn out, drawn, or peaked, and their shoulders aren't slouching. Their natural lines and wrinkles are not as pronounced, and those signs of age do not draw any particular attention. However, be assured that considerable attention is paid to those people who aren't sleeping well. Their ghoulish appearance says it all.

A lack of sleep also will affect your energy level, sharpness of mind, and quality of mood. If you don't sleep enough, your body does not rejuvenate—period. Don't think that making up for lost sleep over a weekend corrects the damage that you are imposing. The same principle applies to exercising only on weekends and expecting dramatic results. It will not happen. Of course, on both points, exercise and sleep when you can. It is better than doing nothing at all.

EXERCISE

Let's be candid. Recent statistics cite that seven out of ten Americans do not exercise. The other three are doing it with varying degrees of regularity. It's safe to say that many of us hate scheduled exercise, and many more of us believe that we don't have the time to commit to regular exercise. Then there are those who have tried everything like yoga, kickboxing, running, dance, calisthenics, tennis, skiing, and swimming. Those are the people realizing they should exercise, but take on the latest craze without regularity. They ride the roller-coaster of exercise for a few months, then drop it, and return back to another type of activity when they witness physical changes like weight gain. Sound familiar? Guess what? Factors such as age, before or after health problems, work schedules and environmental changes—all contribute to why we do or do not exercise. Exercise is about being active and maintaining regularity, not keeping up with fads, trends, or weight-loss programs.

There also are some people who reject anything strenuous, particularly when other priorities enter the picture. Exercise becomes what we do on the weekends, if at all—or maybe, we take up a regimen while on vacation. That isn't a good way to go about it, either. Irregular exercise does the following: Whatever the exercise, you escalate the pumping of your heart long enough to improve blood flow and circulation. You move your muscles and encourage oxygen flow. That's a good thing, except for the fact that without the regular escalation and exercising of muscles, there's no improvement in your physical condition. **"Conditioning" implies constant and regular**. Your heart and other muscles don't get *exercised* into good shape if they have had a week to recover and slide back into being out of shape. The result is only a stressing of that organ or muscles, rather than exercising them into stronger and healthier function.

We all are equipped with a body that demands physical activity, and we need to move it to improve it. Without exercise, our bodies are not operating at their best. *Your Life IQ* encourages balance when undertaking physical activity, in order to make that activity beneficial and enjoyable.

Why Do We Need to Exercise?

We all have heard it before, but here's the bottom line why we need to exercise: Exercise will reduce stress, and improve your heart and circulation. You will begin to have more energy, and will feel less fragile and fatigued. Strength and vitality will reappear. Endorphins will enter your brain and alleviate some of the more cloudy moods you have been experiencing. Stamina will enable you to do more, and your body will tone and look better. Chances are heavily in your favor that you will lose weight, provided you don't overdo it with eating, falsely rewarding yourself for your progress. Also, digestion and other bodily functions will improve. With renewed confidence, you will begin to look and feel better—opening the door to change and its possibilities.

The Practical Side to Exercise

If you've been a couch potato all your life, or have simply given up exercise, don't fret. There is a simple, common-sense approach to exercise, no matter who you are. Before you do anything, start by standing up straight! Good posture is the beginning of self-confidence, and it allows the air you're breathing to be better utilized, therefore, improving your energy level and attitude. **The goal of physical activity will be to condition, improve, and love your body.**

Choose the type of exercise you wish to integrate. If you don't know what you would like to do, ask the following question: Is there any type of exercise to which you gravitate? Remember to be realistic about what you are able and not able to do with exercise. Exercise choices always look good from the outside, but if you haven't had a regimen in years, you should initially consider less strenuous exercise. Exercise can be changed and upgraded anytime, as long as the goal is to remain active.

Ask: How much time do I really have to dedicate? Generally speaking, thirty minutes three times a week is a great start. If you think a gym environment is best for you, will you really go to that gym as planned, or will a membership be unused? What are you really trying to accomplish? The goal is to move and be active; the rest is of minimal importance.

Let's start with the common sense behind exercise, regardless of whether or not you are a beginner, advanced, or someone who may simply detest exercise. Try the following three disciplines: **Do simple stretching, bending and walking.** No excuses—if you have a body, this is the minimum we ought to be doing. It's easy. Do it at home. Do a little at a time, start with a mere five minutes, but know that whatever you do—it is for a lifetime.

Start walking. It sounds crazy, but many of us barely move, going from the car or public transportation to the office and then back again. Walking is an all-around good aerobic workout and builds bone density. We all know how to do it, and we can maintain or alter the routine at our own pace. Walking, as an exercise, can last a lifetime, no matter how old we become. As you improve, gradually increase the distance and walk more vigorously. If you have only half an hour a day, walk as fast as you can. That half an hour walk will soon turn into fifteen minutes, as you strengthen your ability. At that point, you will have enough time to add on more distance. This routine and attitude holds true for those already exercising. If you are presently comfortable in a routine of exercising, be sure to integrate balance and moderation to your routine.

Practice the following: Always warm up before exercise, and warm down afterward. You may want to gently move, swing, and stretch your body. It prevents that initial soreness we feel in our muscles, and protects us from injury. Regardless of your exercise selection, be consistent and dedicated. Try mixing up exercise routines, particularly if you play a sport that utilizes some, but not all, muscles. Just like with food, diversity makes things interesting and fun.

Just in case exercise is something you cannot consider, reflect on the following: Housework and any type of walking counts. Chasing after your kids counts too. Walking to work and climbing stairs is also a way to stay in shape. Cooking, moving around the kitchen, lifting groceries, and breathing deeply counts too. **It is only inactivity that is unhealthy.** Let's throw in a brief reminder about your mindset. Attitude is everything when it comes to exercise. Forget the excuses, and just accept that it must be done. Your body and health is your responsibility, so don't shrug it off by expecting doctors and medical professionals to stay on your tail when it comes to optimal body balance.

Here's some common sense for a good attitude that may work for people who frequently have tried exercising, but couldn't remain consistent: "You eat every day, you exercise every day." How can this be? Let those words ring in your ears every time you pursue a course of exercise. How can you do it every day? Instantly, it should make you think about what you're doing, and how much time it will take. Without a doubt, you won't have time to overdo it, so it better be efficient and thoughtful, just like everything else in your life. It also will become a pleasant habit that doesn't turn you off because the time you have allotted works into your schedule every day. This daily goal calls for daily motivation. That motivation will be helpful when you are filled with those excuses that try to seduce you away from exercising. If it's every day, you don't have the option of interchanging days when it's not convenient. When the attitude is three times a week or less, you can continually find ways to bypass exercising.

Daily exercise translates into not noticing how frequently you are exercising, as well as not feeling stressed because you missed the prearranged day for exercise. The result of such an attitude is that when time does not permit—or you go on vacation, or you just feel you deserve some long awaited rest—you take it, without guilt. Your exercise routine stands a higher chance of succeeding, when you know that every day is a day you can return to your schedule. If you pursue an exercise like walking, excuses will be harder to find.

There is one more component to a good attitude. Just like eating healthier foods first requires focus, so does your exercise. If it truly becomes a lifetime commitment, your state of mind is one that accepts exercise as something permanent. This will replace the state of mind that wants to conjure up excuses like an impertinent child. Without the lifetime commitment state of mind, if you do take one day off, it soon becomes two, then three, then you stop altogether. Now, those of you who can maintain a faithful regimen of four to five times a week, we applaud you—and keep it up! For the rest of us, attitude will have to be everything!

FINDING YOUR BODY BALANCE

All of your choices should be implemented only when you truly are ready to make a lifetime commitment. That way, your mind is clear on what the objective is. Don't feel deprived or constrained when undertaking new regimens. Eat fresh, and eat fewer calories. Eat when you're hungry. Exercise regularly. A healthy body is not only about losing weight and looking better, but also improving overall health from the inside out. Maintaining body balance produces quality living, and unlocks our natural healing ability.

Everything you do in your life will have a positive or negative affect on your body. When your body is out of balance, it lacks energy and becomes vulnerable to illness. Eating healthier foods and exercising regularly unleashes your healing ability. You are less prone to getting colds, and your odds of contracting illness decreases. Your healing ability readily is usable when you are in balance. It's like your internal compass. Unless you locate and utilize it, you won't even know where it is. *Stress* affects every function in your body, including your healing ability, and exercise is the physical aspect of stress reduction. Stress management will be covered in depth in the chapter of the *Mind*, as most physical symptoms of stress originate in the mind.

After you've made a commitment to better health, take a good look at yourself. Look at the positives, but be acquainted with your negatives. Why? We all have both, but for improving our life IQ, we are interested in enhancing the positives. Never focus attention on the negatives, or you will become negative. Don't be fooled; even the people who physically appear to "have it all," don't. Perfection does not exist. Know that we all have our pluses and minuses, and our job is to maintain balance.

If the preceding sounds a bit idealistic, have you ever met a wonderful person who is so comfortable in their own shoes, although he/she is not quite the image of a model type? These people possess an inherent attitude that goes a long way in terms of appearance.

They exude so much positive energy that it completely overshadows physical appearances. Be on the alert. People initially may notice the exterior, but once your "energy" appears, will they see positive or negative? Which would you like to be, and whose company would you prefer? It's also a great idea to practice good grooming and cleanliness. Paying attention to your appearance speaks volumes about your self-esteem. Take pride in yourself, because who you are is evidenced by how you take care of your body!

When it comes to our health and body, we must continue to challenge what is cited as "normal" and "acceptable." Reject the notion that age automatically brings on illness or acceptable versions of inadequate health. Do not accept given standards of safety and so called acceptable amounts of any chemicals—either in your food, water, or skincare before personal investigation. Complement your decision-making by listening to your gut feelings.

Relax long-standing rules and expectations, and begin to eliminate the pressure to conform by continuing to educate yourself. Knowledge empowers you to want to do more. *YOUR LIFE IQ* **encourages supplemental reading and investigation**. After you've mastered a discipline and it becomes second nature in your daily routine, read up on other aspects of your health. When you have built the foundation to maintaining balance, you will be ready to absorb more difficult challenges of integrating healthy habits.

Be open-minded about alternative medicine and treatments. **Remember, there is more than one way to do anything**. Become accustomed to looking at any illness, even a cold, as having a root to the problem. Don't just take cold medications and accept that is was "just a cold." You caught a cold because your immune system was off. Ask why and how. Stress is a good place to start, along with an honest review of your recent health habits.

Know that medications suppress symptoms. That "suppression" in your body can compromise the functioning of some organs, particularly the liver, and leads to side effects of the medications. It behooves us to understand the dangers of medication, as well as the cost/benefit of symptom alleviation.

The bottom line for maintaining body balance is that it enhances life extension and the quality of our experience. We will benefit from the anti-aging effects of a healthy body by looking younger and feeling better. The effects of a good lifestyle will unlock our natural healing ability, along with positive energy, and will keep disease and illness at bay. Make reasonable choices, practice patience, and take personal responsibility for all of your health decisions.

And whatever you do, make a lifetime commitment!

IV.

MIND

Holistic thinking must be instilled into our lives in order to promote balance in any of the three components, including the mind. Our field of energy (all made up of subatomic particles), encompasses our bodies, minds, and spirits. They all are connected and interrelated. Our mind (housing thoughts and feelings), and our body (matter) are alike, and it is helpful to accept that the vitality and strength we seek in our body also should be sought for the mind.

Mind-Body Medicine is holistic medicine because in takes into consideration the interaction between the mind, body and spirit. It considers mental, emotional, social, and experiential factors, and how these factors can affect your overall health. "The concept that the mind is important in health and illness dates back to ancient times. In the West, the notion that mind and body were separate began during the Renaissance and Enlightenment eras. Increasing numbers of scientific and technological discoveries furthered this split and led to an emphasis on disease-based models, pathological changes, and external cures. The role of mind and belief in health and illness began to re-enter

Western health care in the 20th century..." US Department of Health and Human Services, NIH Research Portfolio Online Reporting Tools - Mind-Body Medicine Practices in Complementary and Alternative Medicine.

We then should consider that our minds possess an extraordinary amount of power. As with our bodies, there is an optimal experience for all of our thoughts and feelings. Those thoughts and feelings impact our bodies, thus contributing to the level and type of energy we exude as human beings. The mind should be looked upon not as abstract and inaccessible, but as a powerful tool that fuels your entire existence. The brain is the organ that transmits our thoughts and feelings, and the quality of those thoughts and feelings—or lack of it—will depend on how we care for our mind. We have a tendency to disregard its caretaking because we cannot see the mind, but the same kind of attention must be paid to our minds that we pay to our bodies.

As related to our essence and inner core, we possess an individual system that is unique. Since birth, our experiences, circumstances, and events are like no one else's, and incorporating this understanding will cause us to appreciate our special way of living and thinking. All of who we are positively can impact our choices, provided we are aware of our individual influence to consciously create the quality of life we desire.

Who are we, exactly? Each of us has an individual and

unique system that makes us distinct from all others. We differ by our sensory capacities, intelligence, physical abilities, social skills, knowledge and experience, and finally, energy. The *Self* (who we are) represents the essential qualities that make a person one of a kind. The challenge is to define, expand and utilize these qualities. Only through knowing the self, can we attain true success and well-being. Sounds simple, but our essence is complex and multidimensional. The fact that every human being is made up of physical, mental, emotional and spiritual dimensions presents the challenge of putting those dimensions into balance. However, if we evolve into our truest potential, we will expose the dynamic quality of who we are—to reveal an energetic and vibrant being. If we make a commitment to expand personally, in a way, *exercise* our mind, we are able to do better than before. We become more effective and organized. We increase our capacity for accomplishment by experiencing increased energy, enthusiasm and confidence, and we begin to experience a desire to discover and know more.

Accept that we live on earth to learn and grow. We are here to experience life and its possibilities, whatever they may be. There will be good and bad experiences. We must dissect them to understand where our learning lies. There will be trial and error. When it comes to the journey of life, we cannot escape making mistakes, even outright blunders. However, if you are in balance, crises will be better managed. You will weather life's storms while still navigating toward your desired success.

A strong, healthy mind—a mind without clutter—
embraces all experiences to the fullest and naturally
protects us when times are difficult. A strong mind is
positive. It is in a state of peace and tranquility, and
has the ability to produce that state at its will. **A
healthy mind commands sustained attention to any
goal or desire**. It has the ability consciously to shift
and create the transformation to positive energy and
peace. That free, uncluttered mind has the power of
concentration. It possesses expansive insight and
awareness to reveal all possibilities when in search for
solutions. A type of liberation exists, a balance of
emotions with the freedom from limitations. All choices
are conscious, not unconscious.

Conscious choices are:
- Evaluated
- Optimal
- Informed
- Deliberate

Unconscious choices are:
- Impulsive
- Indifferent & mediocre
- Ignorant & oblivious
- Unintentional

Weaker minds won't be of much help when making
decisions, battling illness, or undertaking other
challenges that require a positive mindset. Unhealthy
minds have a tendency to make choices

unconsciously, which create undesirable and complicated situations. A negative mindset delineates pessimism and fear, which curtails and prevents achievement. Worse, this type of thinking makes us more susceptible to disease. We can talk ourselves into anything, including all that is bad or negative. Try telling yourself that you are feeling sick, tired, or stressed day after day. Most assuredly, you eventually will wake up sicker, more tired, and more stressed than you actually imagined. The same is true for the person who, day after day, insists that he or she will experience a wonderful day. He/she most definitely will. We all manifest our destiny, but we need to understand that when our destiny arrives and the way it is packaged, will be determined by our mindset.

For clarity's sake, manifesting your destiny means the following: *You,* and you alone, are responsible for creating the reality in which you live. Simply, you can alter and change your reality if you so choose. That holds true for all of your thoughts and feelings. This statement is not some quixotic commentary. The subatomic particles we mentioned earlier possess an organizing power that influences how we see and perceive all things around us. Our thoughts and feelings organize those particles, so know that you are in charge. Imagine the possibilities when your mind is fit and strong. The result of that type of strong attention and positive focus will unleash extraordinary events and achievements. We have all heard the success stories. For example, you may be experiencing negative circumstances, such as having no job and no money. It will take time to alter and change that circumstance, but you *can* change it. Depending on what you want and how you think, will depend on whether or not you attain it. If you continually feel negative about the job market, you will not see where the exceptions exist, and you will not act creatively when seeking a job. That thinking will quash all hope. On the other hand, if you know that the market truly is limiting, it just might inspire you to be more proactive when searching for a job—perhaps going into a commercial building and entering each office of business, on each floor, to inquire about a potential job. Eventually, you will walk into an office where, if they cannot help you, they will make a recommendation as to who will—provided, of course, that you don't stroll in disheveled and unprepared.

Don't be fooled into thinking that you do not possess the kind of power it takes to make big changes, let alone achieve big dreams. The power of the mind has been scientifically documented. Niels Bohr, considered the father of quantum physics, tells us that the observer cannot observe anything without changing what he sees. How can that be? The subatomic particles that make us who we are, is only empty space that is filled once we focus our attention. That concept further was explored through a series of well-documented experiments. Princeton researchers Brenda I. Dunne and Robert G. Jahn have established that our minds, as well as our intent, can alter the outcome of events. If the topic of quantum physics intrigues you, in relation to how it affects our daily living, an easy start toward learning more can be achieved by watching the film, *What the Bleep?*

Accept that the mind is a powerful tool. That tool is responsible for every thought, intention, and action for every single moment of the day. Is your mindset and outlook in life, positive or negative? If your thoughts, intentions, and actions are negative, the reactions toward you will be negative. For instance, you imagine that people on the street only have an interest in making your life more difficult when they grimace in your presence, bump into you, or don't say excuse me when passing through a crowd. Eventually, that negative perception will attract major run-ins with people, who will, make your life difficult. On the other hand, this doesn't mean that if you always practice kindness and kind thoughts, intentions, and actions, you never will encounter the thugs of the world. However, it does reduce those incidents dramatically, and they no longer will have a negative impact on your energy and you.

Let's explore another example. You are in a restaurant and after fifteen minutes, the waiter still forgets to bring you water. Responding negatively, you decide that he must be stupid or incompetent, and you become angry and tell him so. There was no negative intention toward you, yet you invited a confrontation because of your own way of interpreting the situation. Even if he truly is incompetent, why not let it go, instead? Was it worth the angry feeling that filled your body and mind with negativity, to point out his supposed incompetence? And further, why do you care? Perhaps you might consider that somewhere inside you, dissatisfaction of self is lingering, and the anger is popping up as a valuable signal to address something about you and your perceptions.

A less obvious reaction of a negative mindset is the continued preoccupation and "worrying" about what other people are doing or thinking, prior to them doing anything. A chronic energy waster, you spend what starts off as good energy turned bad by first guessing, then worrying about other people's reactions—instead of spending that good energy on things you actually can influence. Why is there a sole preoccupation with negative responses? Why not spend that time "preoccupied" with the good things to come?

Another typical example that produces negativity is when people need to stand up for how they feel. Worrying about hurting someone else is the classic response of people with lower self-esteem. It's a great excuse packaged as compassion, whereas such people really are more concerned about being uncomfortable because they might have to discuss their feelings—and the possibility that those feelings might hurt someone really is not the concern. They hide behind compassion, truly fearful of bad reactions and are avoiding confrontations. In all of those situations, the only thing one really has to worry about is how the message should be delivered.

There are many negative behavior patterns, and it is safe to say that we all know the difference between positive and negative. All you have to do is observe how you feel during the course of the day. When do you feel discomfort, or when are you agitated? Among all the people in your life, who inspires positive thoughts, and who inspires negative? Observe how you handle small annoyances, let alone, crises in your life. Know that all these feelings matter when it comes to overall balance and quality living.

For mental acuity, you will have to work on yourself and your behavior to discover who you are, and to discover your rightful path. **Don't make the mistake of thinking that somehow, you can bypass the process of personal growth and achieve success**. There is not a single individual who has nothing to learn, regardless of his or her age, education and experience. It does not matter at what stage you are in your life—you always will have something to learn. You also will have to be proactive in stress management as it is the number one problem creating energy shortages in your life. Stress is toxic to the body, mind and spirit, and significantly can compromise your overall health by inducing bio-chemical reactions that further break down the health of your body. All of those negative feelings and chemicals create psychological stresses. What is the number one killer these days? Stress. Stress "wakes up" weaknesses in your body and brings the onset of illness. The body is not separate from the mind, and it is helpful to understand that when you are sick, your mind is suffering as well. Caroline Myss, PhD. and a medical intuitive, illustrates this point quite impressively. Based on fifteen years of study in energy medicine, she shows how every illness corresponds to a pattern of emotional and psychological stresses, beliefs, and attitudes that have influenced corresponding areas of the human body.

Personal growth will include the examination of your belief systems. Breaking down belief systems opens the door to change. **Your beliefs drive your behavior.** When we begin to investigate our behavior, we begin to understand how we truly think and feel. Our mind assimilates what we *will* it to think and believe. *That* determines how we will communicate with ourselves and others. When you evaluate what you believe, which truly is an exercise of evaluating conditioning, you will be able to distinguish which of your choices are conscious or unconscious, and which are positive or negative. That knowledge empowers us to change negative behavior patterns. In knowing your belief systems, you will know the self, and you begin to unlock the gateway to awareness—awareness of your attitudes and values—and which ones hamper the success you desire. Success, of any kind, evolves with personal growth because we become more responsible and more self-reliant. We begin to aspire for higher achievements (because we believe that we can), and thus, begin to live higher standards and higher values. So, how many of us have made a commitment to practice personal growth as a lifetime exercise? If you fall into the category of not having made a commitment, you may want to reconsider that decision.

Current statistics on the website of the National

Institute of Mental Health (NIMH) list a continued rise in the spectrum of illnesses associated with mental disorders, anxiety, compulsiveness and depression. The percentage of Americans suffering with mental health problems is staggering. We need to consider the following: If we ignore the caretaking of the mind, are we developing a lack of mental control by allowing social and cultural woes, and dissatisfaction with our lives, to create more ailments that require medication? Are we so stressed out that we abandon the necessity of a holistic approach with our mental health choices, and instead, create a habitual reliance on drugs? We need to question why there is a lack of advertising and mass-marketing encouraging and steering us toward "exercising" the mind into better health. Most of us would agree that our mental health is compromised sporadically throughout our lifetime—when we face difficult challenges or undergo personal trauma. Isn't it time to safeguard our mental health by taking control and doing what it takes to strengthen this influential component?

As with our bodies, we need to take responsibility for our mental health. Common sense says that today's rise in mental illness does not mean that most of us will become incapacitated. It does imply, however, that a good number of us are quite overwhelmed. Doesn't it seem obvious that we can attribute some of our mental weakness to the high-tech assault in our lifestyles of multi-tasking, information bombardment, and our societal conditioning that defines who and what we should be? Good sense says that we aren't very good at managing our Twenty-first Century stress inducing activities and environments. Taking a vacation used to be the solution that rejuvenated us and erased the year's woes. Now, we are plagued with so much tension and stress that a vacation only serves as a temporary Band-Aid™. A little time off no longer addresses the types of problems we must endure. However, with the integration of positive mental disciplines, our stress can be successfully thwarted with a vibrant mind free of hyper-inflated realities. **There are three disciplines we must work on to produce a healthy and powerful mind:** Personal growth, stress management, and mind maintenance.

PERSONAL GROWTH

"The main cause of our problems is the neglect of the inner life", writes His Holiness, the thirteenth Dalai Lama, a Buddhist monk.

Personal growth is the process of inner discovery, and it is directly related to emotional growth. Many of us spend little, if any, time reflecting on our attitudes or behavior long enough to change them. If we do any reflection, our tendency is to reject or disregard negative emotions for fear that they might open a Pandora's Box, or, we distance ourselves as far away as possible and pretend that nothing needs to be addressed. However, the only thing that we will achieve in dodging this learning will be more negative circumstances and events that will come stronger and harder. Without personal growth, patterns of behavior develop, as will patterns of predictable results. If you are of adult age, this has already happened.

Personal growth does not take place by intellectualizing upheavals and uncomfortable realities. It's a nice start, but it is the underlying emotions that need to be explored. The level of honesty and overall integrity of how we address our feelings leads either to personal growth or stagnation. In the last twenty years, many books have been written to inform us about the emotional quotient. Just like with our IQ (intelligence quotient), we have an EQ that determines our emotional intelligence. And just like when we take care of our IQ by learning and expanding our horizons to better our lives—our EQ requires similar caretaking. Disregarding how we feel in any given situation is to ignore an important component contributing to a loss in our equilibrium.

Crises and emotional upheavals are meant to wake us up and give us a chance to learn. They will come and go throughout our lifetime, so what will matter is how we relate during those experiences. Will we be out of control, in a frenzy or paralyzed, or, will we be steady, alert, and ready to act? We should try not to focus on the "bad" of that experience and how it is disruptive and painful. Instead, we should view that experience as a moment in time when we have something to learn. It may not be easy to integrate at first, but over time, it will take the focus off the actual event to force our thoughts into the exercise of discovering what there is to learn. While the event or circumstance might be negative, the approach is positive, and it is the conscious shifting to positive that we are interested in achieving.

How do we achieve conscious shifting to a positive mindset?

Personal growth always comes with a price tag. It can include the loss of friends, a change in job, or a break-up with a partner. All of these can be extremely painful experiences. That's why most of us avoid deeper introspection—it keeps us away from the hurt that eventually will expose a part of our life that we need to change. We don't like change, want to remain in control, and we create remarkable excuses that steer us clear of emotional upheavals—sometimes we simply pretend that nothing is wrong. Generally speaking, most of us have embarked on some type of personal growth—not by choice, but because certain events cornered us into feeling helpless. Those events had to do with personal loss, something that was taken from us—the death of a loved one, financial disaster, getting fired from a job, or the break-up of a relationship. Do you see the direct connection between life-changing events and the opportunity for personal growth, as a time to learn?

There are good reasons why we want to embark on a road to personal growth. The more you work on yourself, the closer you get to your true self and your rightful path. What is the rightful path? It is what you do best and unlike anyone else. It could be your work, your mothering, or your kindness to others. It could be your generosity, your ability to listen, or your research skills. More likely than not, there will be a combination of abilities specific to you. Personal growth inspires change, and change happens even if you dodge its inevitability. Life guarantees it. The only difference is whether *YOU* decide to enact change, or allow change to happen to you. If you enact it first, you get to make the decision that's most positive and right for you. The other way of doing nothing will allow the forces of the universe to dictate the enormity of that change. Either way, there will be personal growth. You make the decision.

In case you doubt the forces of the universe, quantum physics applies here, as well. Since we already ascertained the mind as a powerful tool, now imagine the enormity of the universe that houses everything and everyone into a massive field of energy. Don't you think that level and variety of power is so exponentially huge, that it can intimidate anything that we can possibly grasp, let alone perceive?

There are two choices in how you approach personal growth, positive and negative. There's no in between. If you want to develop your life IQ, all you do will have to sway toward the positive. Again, it's like physical exercise and what you eat. It is a quality decision for a lifetime, and it takes a conscious effort. You're going to have to keep it up. And just like for your body health, your mental health commitments will be challenged by moments when you fall short, unable to remain positive in dire circumstances, so much so that bypassing a positive attitude will be impossible. Always give yourself some slack, and get back to a positive attitude when you are ready. None of us is perfect.

As with the body, you will have to change your habits, and for this chapter, those habits will be referred to as behavior. Do not confuse behavior with personality. Personality is what you are born with—those inherent qualities you possess as an individual—and behavior is learned. Do not pressure yourself with unrealistic expectations of suddenly becoming a "Zen-like" individual with profound inner peace, or a flower child who espouses love, because we all are vastly different. What's good for one person, is not good for the other. Strong mental health will not be achieved overnight. **Personal growth lasts a lifetime** because as we grow, our perspectives change, our circumstances change, and depending on how we live, will depend on what we want, what we do, whom we love.

Continued attention to personal growth creates an ease of discovering who you really are. Being who you are requires the least effort, thus your energy is more efficient. There's no calculated energy involved if you are who you are. If you're busy holding up that mask of what you want people to see and interpret, you meet up with the energy of resistance. That resistant energy is created by *the you* on the outside that resists *the you* on the inside. Resistance in any form requires twice the effort and wastes good energy. However, the real problem with resisting is that you expel negative energy. Why should we care?

Negative energy produces negative emotional responses such as anger, dissatisfaction, depression, and a whole slew of other fear-based emotions. Fear in any form can paralyze you, and prevents you from reaching your potential. That mask is a result of fear, perhaps a feeling of inadequacy, or a desire for approval or love. It is an attempt to cover up insecurities we are desperate to hide. Fear blocks your mental circuits when it comes to making a decision that will make you happy. Justification will materialize to support those negative notions that resulted from fear, just like it does when you consider that same choice in the positive. **Only positive energy breeds optimism, satisfaction, all possibilities, and no limitations on what you can do.**

Countless books and therapists exist to help us along the path of personal growth. Should you wish to pursue them, please do. *Your Life IQ* is not meant to be a substitute for further learning, or a substitute for seeking the advice of a medical professional, should one be needed. However, many of us don't have the resources to dedicate to a formalized course of personal growth, or the time to delve into the array of books on psychology, self-help, social sciences and philosophy. There is a common sense approach, so let's begin. There are three basic steps to personal growth.

1. Eliminate all bad attitudes and bad emotional habits, including those that encourage self-imposed limitations.
2. Ask the question: Do I react out of fear or love? Resolve the differences.
3. Get to know yourself, and make sure you stop the denial.

No matter where you start, you must eliminate bad attitudes and bad emotional habits such as poor self-concepts. That means you need to purge all negative feelings, especially those that reinforce negative beliefs about who you are. Bad attitudes and bad emotional habits single-handedly can strangle your success in life, and will affect your overall well-being. They diminish your innate abilities by creating self-doubt, rejection, inferiority, and disappointment. **Bad attitudes and poor self-concepts distort reality.** They make us feel that little is possible, immovable obstacles exist, and that no one is on our side. A defeatist attitude can ensue, and leads us into negative second thoughts about who we are and what we want to do. This negative questioning snowballs into the destruction of our hopes and dreams, finally affecting out health.

The words "limits and limitations" should evaporate from your vocabulary because that's exactly what you'll get when it comes to achieving dreams. You are as limited as you make yourself. Ever hear of those amazing stories of people with disabilities who do supposedly miraculous things? They are not just lucky, or have a talent better than anyone comparable. Those people are staunch believers in themselves and their abilities, rather than their limitations or disabilities. Obstacles always will exist for those who wish to succeed. Why? It's the crazy natural law of the universe that asks, "Are you sure you really want this?" Then you are tested and tested until it is easier and easier to just give up. DON'T—this process is meant to eliminate those who say they want success versus those who truly expect to have it. Finally, repeat as often as possible: **I can vs. I can't**. Scream it, if you have to.

As with all three components of body, mind and spirit, conditioning plays an important role in our mindset. Our mindset reflects what we believe, and when it is negative, negative behavior patterns exist. Without a doubt, we all have developed at least one, but usually several, negative feelings that have turned into negative emotional patterns, referred to as schemas in the profession of psychology. These patterns of behavior affect what we notice, how we interpret things, how we make decisions and how we act. However, one need not get caught up in understanding the technical phraseology to improve mentally. Simply, think about what circumstances cause you to become angry, frustrated, disappointed, or inadequate. At what moments do you overreact to small annoyances? Do you over- or under-eat when you feel emotional discomfort? **Our goal is to change and alter negative responses to the positive**. Positive behavior and positive changes only can lead to positive benefits, and the same is true for the negative.

To eliminate poor self-concepts (what we believe about our self) and bad attitudes, we must begin with investigating and recognizing what they are. If you have no idea what they are or where to start, try listening to your internal dialogue. When trouble hits, do you hear internal voices telling you to get angry and vengeful, making you feel less deserving, or explaining why you will never be good enough, no matter what you do? Do you hear a chattering of downside opinions regarding your abilities, and why what you might want is out of reach? Conversely, do you prop yourself up so far above others that your attitude of superiority attracts a slew of negative battering, and leaves you dumbfounded as to why you haven't achieved your goals? These are the voices of criticism, dissatisfaction, entitlement, and perfection. They never give any slack, and make you feel powerless, weak, and like a failure. Without a doubt, you will feel defeated, and without options. Start by smothering those nasty voices. They impose a constant preoccupation with negativity, thus distracting us from finding, let alone, integrating, any positive solutions.

Make an inflexible commitment to let go of bad emotions. They are distracting and keep you away from solutions. Do you ever know the type of people who go on and on about their problems, chewing your ear off for months on end, and despite all the solutions you suggest, they still do nothing but harp on the same problem? Well, that's the distraction that keeps us from actually moving on. Why would we intentionally do such a thing? The simple answer is to avoid change by learning. It's harder to say, "Gee, I have to change my behavior," than it is to bludgeon the person or source of discontent. **The focus should be on the solution, not the problem**.

For instance, thinking that you are not good enough has infected many of us; it is a good example of a poor self-concept. In a society that worships big money and grandiosity, many of us feel that most things are unattainable. This is a bad emotional habit. Treat this bad emotional habit or any other that is negative, as a dragon that must be slain to the death. Every time you hear that voice, or feel incapable, visualize a sword that will annihilate that dragon into smithereens. If you must, take pleasure in his demise. This suggestion is only that, a suggestion. If you find other ways to vanquish these demons, use them! The point is to accept and understand that these habits must be broken in order to achieve any of your goals—including that of being happy. Happiness comes from within. When you allow negative internal dialogue to find refuge in your mind, it will submerge you into chronic discontent. Your mindset needs to change to one of **dedication and commitment to a positive you.** It is your continued path toward balance.

Don't get caught up in *who* made you feel poorly. You're only shifting blame—and *that* also is a bad emotional habit. If you have to tie your hands, or put duct tape over your mouth to avoid negative responses you know are destructive, DO IT! Prior to habitual personal growth, we can't always dissect why we are reacting with hostility or subjugation, or other negative feelings, but we do know that we are. You **can** help *that*, and the mere decision to halt that behavior will begin to shift your consciousness toward thinking again, and considering another alternative. **Force yourself to find positive alternatives**. They are there, even if you reject them. Know that every time you say that you cannot help a negative response, you are choosing not to change. How is that working for you? Are you carefree, happy, and getting what you want?

Only you are responsible for your thoughts, intentions, and actions, and *excusing* yourself because someone took the first step toward a negative response, is an outright refusal to accept your responsibility. Conscious or not, you are stuck with negativity. That negativity will cause you further disruption and discomfort by infringing on your mood and physically permeating your cells. Will your choice be positive or negative?

The process of change begins with a commitment to *treat you* as the most important person on the planet. That means you will not postpone personal growth. Your thoughts need to be those of respect, admiration, and love for you. When you matter to yourself, you maintain an identity that cannot be penetrated by negativity or negative people. A natural barrier develops that inspires confidence, fearlessness, and an ability to embrace change and all possibilities.

Let's start with one of the most overused phrases in all

of self-help. You are the most important person on the planet. Tiresome as many platitudes may be, you need to consider yourself a priority because if you take good care of yourself, you will be of better service to you and others. You will have more to give because you will be in better standing with yourself. Filtered a bit more, it means you are of no use to you and your loved ones if you are on overload! Automatically, some of you may have gone into the reasons why taking "real" care of yourself isn't realistic. Perhaps there are excuses of time constraints, someone else's needs superseding your own, or finances. Know that this is the moment you need to say, "I can versus I can't."

If you break down what respect, admiration and love may mean in relation to how you feel about yourself, the following questions will surface.

- **Respect** – How do I judge myself? What is my opinion of myself? Do I have high, medium, or low self-esteem?
- **Admiration** – Do I appreciate or look up to myself? Do I admire myself in the same way I admire others?
- **Love** – How do I honor myself? Do I take time just for taking care of me? Do I love myself enough to do what is right by me? Do I love who I am?

Without respect, admiration, and love for yourself, you not only will hand yourself over to others and their ways, but also will project the opposite of respect, admiration, and love. Do you ever hear people complaining about not being treated with respect, or why no one appreciates their achievements, qualities, or loves them? Why do you suppose that is? It always is because they DO NOT treat themselves with respect, admiration, or love, almost begging for mistreatment. A positive mindset will allow you to respect yourself enough to stand up for yourself, as well as attract the reality of respect, admiration, and love. Knowing that you are important is the first step to acknowledging love for the self. If your field of energy is negative—a field of energy without respect, admiration, and love—be prepared for negativity.

Falling into negative emotional patterns that perpetuate a lack of respect, admiration, and love for oneself generally are masked by excuses of need: "My children need me to," or, "My husband or wife needs me to," or chronically volunteering, "OK, I'll do it," or excuses of perfection such as, "Only I can do it correctly," or, "If I don't do it, it won't get done." As time constraints strangle you into overdoing it, leaving you resentful and angry, you then are filled with negative responses. This attracts negative responses from others, when perhaps, one little thing did not get done. Rather than asking, let alone demanding help, or insisting that you need time to yourself and taking it, you cower into the "woe is me" position. This can render you truly feeling helpless and without options. Know that it is *your* mindset that imposes a screwy reality that **YOU** are choosing not to change. Before we embark on the basic steps to enact personal growth, try to adhere to the following practices:

Even the WORST of circumstances has a silver lining. Look for a silver lining until you find it. Make it your mission. The question to ask is, what am I supposed to learn? How can I change? How can I turn this bad event around into something positive? As we all know, it isn't always easy to find a "bright side" when stripped of a loved one in the most horrific of circumstances, or losing our entire net worth in a day. However, a positive mindset acts like a weeding process in life. Before the demons of negativity awake to strangle our progress with misery, hopelessness, and illness, a positive mindset reaches out to force positive change quickly.

Keep your dreams away from those who are unable to support your effort. The last thing you need is someone to drag you down and pull you dangerously close to self-doubt and destructive thinking. Don't look at setbacks as failure, and don't let anyone convince you that setbacks *are* failure. Setbacks are a part of the process to success, in a way, a type of preparation for when you finally do succeed.

Do not depend on anything external. That means, do not depend on people and things outside of your inner self. This does not mean to disregard the opinions or guidance of others, but it does mean to ultimately rely and depend on your own ability to discern what is good for you, and what is not. For instance, you may be faced with the reality that your marriage is over—and you know it. Many around you are still urging you to try again. Their opinions and advice is sound, but YOU have determined that you must move on, despite the difficulty. What should you do? Do you follow the advice of others, hoping new events might arrive to somehow change your mind about the decision you know you should be making? No one knows what is better for you than you. **Trust your inner core** when it tells you what to do, and know that this process is related directly to being who you are. Although the action of deciding to divorce equates to emotional difficulty, that process will lead you to your better self—including the possibility of a better relationship. Again, our conditioning and bad emotional habits are multi-layered and have prevented us from becoming our true selves. Therefore, we are predisposed to not achieving what we want. In this case, you want a more fulfilling relationship, and avoiding divorce keeps you spiraling emotionally, closing the door to positive change. When you are your true self, there is no calculation, no energy wasted, and you automatically liberate good energy and feelings. It is through that liberation of good energy and feelings that we improve our life IQ.

The opposite of good energy and good feelings is fear. Fear encompasses a lot of twisted emotions like worry, anxiety, panic, frustration, and depression. It also pertains to feelings of angst, disgust, distress, guilt and shame. You can't find your natural path or harmony if you're caught up in those destructive emotions. As said before, conditioning is responsible for us feeling and believing that we need to satisfy the perspectives of others. Choosing a perspective other than your own, is guaranteed failure—but let's redefine failure. **Failure should be defined as not starting and not trying**. Repeat it a billion times, if you have to. Failure is never getting started, and never trying. The reason it is important to redefine the meaning of failure is because if we continue to consider failure as not achieving, accomplishing, or succeeding in a particular task, WE WILL NEVER TRY. Why? We will not attempt to pursue our dreams or follow our feelings because of the fear of making a mistake, or having to explain why what we tried did not work out. This thinking points to our conditioning of satisfying others and *their* idea of what is right for us.

Distinguishing between what YOU want and what OTHERS want for you, must be ascertained. This is important to understand because it appears and reappears several times throughout life. If you're fortunate enough to know what you want from childhood on, and are able to attain it and contribute positively, marvelous! Most of us don't, so we're left in the confused category. The typical concern is, "I don't know what I want," or perhaps, we have a list of fifty things, and don't know where to begin. This means it's time to embark on an expedition toward personal growth. You can't avoid it. And if you're filled with compulsions, it's time for a change, and change leads to personal growth. You will have to analyze yourself as best you can and determine where you need to make changes, and where you hope to. No one is perfect, and again, these things will be worked on for a lifetime. No one changes overnight, or begins to practice positive thinking after having spent too much time in self-doubt having sought the approval of others.

Getting to know "you" requires the conscious peeling away of crusty layers that have built up over a lifetime. It is an unraveling of your emotions, how you feel, what you like and dislike in yourself and others, and what reactions you undertake in given circumstances and situations—particularly those that unsettle your mind. Do you frequently experience turbulent feelings of worry, fear, anger, frustration, or hatred? With absolute honesty, do you know the sources of your feelings and behavior—good and bad? Why should we care?

The reason we all care is because somehow, somewhere in our lives, we feel dissatisfied and aren't getting what we want. It doesn't matter how small or large a goal we imagine, it still is out of reach. Perhaps frequently we are second guessing our parenting skills, or our ability to get promoted. Maybe we can't find the *right* partner. Maybe we are just fidgety about where we are in life, a bit confused and lost, or maybe nothing we are doing is making any sense. Are we emotionally distancing ourselves, or criticizing those around us? Are we experiencing insomnia, weight gain, or depression? Welcome to the world of personal growth.

Here are the basic ways to begin and/or continue the process of personal growth. The goal is to prompt a better understanding or yourself and your actions. Choose a quiet time to reflect upon and analyze your emotions. Sit or lie comfortably and begin to dedicate a consistent schedule for this process. Slow your normal pace. Don't answer the phone, cook or clean, or listen to music—those are all distracting activities, and the idea is to integrate *mindfulness* to your thinking. Pay attention to your thoughts and pattern of thinking. What discomfort pops up? Think about what and who bothers you. What are the reasons—where does that thinking progress? **HONESTLY investigate your emotions**, and begin to acknowledge and recognize your difficulties. In reflecting upon a situation, think about how you felt and what you did. Where did your responsibility lie? Are your reactions beyond reproach? Nobody's are, so keep thinking and looking for your responsibility.

THE ART OF DENIAL

All over the world, denial is an amazingly elusive and frequently practiced art form. As intelligent and reasoning human beings, we spend half of our time rationalizing what the other half is doing. It justifies, explains, and absolves us in our decision-making and choices. All we have to do is successfully target our goal, then brilliantly package it with socially acceptable reasoning to declare ourselves *right* in what we do.

We all do it. When we are children we follow, and mimic those around us in order to fit in. As adults, that pattern of behavior doesn't readily disappear, but what does improve is our ability to perpetuate automatic responses to what's acceptable and what is not. This continues to validate why we need to break conditioning and evaluate our beliefs, and why we need to work on personal growth. Both bring us closer to our spirit, which defines who we really are.

Denial is tough to recognize because it is defined with contradiction. Denial is ever so near when you've got too many people around you saying the same, unflattering comment, and you flatly reject their observation. If you are losing friends and partners over an issue and/or behavior, and finding quick replacements with those who only agree with you, you are in denial. If you think no one understands, or you don't comprehend why no one but you sees what's right, you are in denial. If your tendency is to hang up the phone, or storm out of a room when confronted, you are in denial. The more tepid and less obvious version of denial is when you cut yourself off emotionally, in order to avoid feeling. Deeply inside, you know what you are feeling, but run from it to avoid confrontation of that difficult feeling. Denial is a strange see-saw of opposing perspectives, and it is easy to defy the perspective that is least flattering. Just remember that the mind is a powerful tool, and it is quite effective when it comes to camouflaging negativity.

Personal growth allows for the diffusion of denial as you slowly unravel the layers that, initially, blur your vision. Do your best not to go into denial by rejecting what seem like crazy observations, because only you will be the recipient of that unevaluated choice. If you shut down and become emotionally distant, you shut down your own possibilities. Change will not be possible—and perhaps, that's exactly what you are avoiding. If you become stressed during your review of an event, take a "time out" and come back to that exploration another time. Answers always will surface to enlighten you when the time is right. Always be patient, and bear in mind that it is impossible to rush personal growth.

WHAT QUESTIONS SHOULD I ASK?

Ask: What is my behavior, good and bad? Do I know the sources of my behavior, good and bad? Observe your discomfort and try to find the root. Don't rush or pressure yourself, and don't fall into the habit of blaming the root, which usually is a person or event. THEY are not responsible for your behavior. Your behavior may have been the result, but only you behave the way you behave. No one forces you, and it is solely your choice. Please keep in mind that "behavior" refers to all negative behavior. This includes silent, negative emotions, such as choosing not to stand up for your feelings and building resentment, people pleasing, harboring feelings of inadequacy, failure, selfishness, inferiority, and hostility. Outwardly manifested or not, negative feelings are negative feelings.

Ask: What events have impacted my life? No matter how big or how small, what are they, and can you face them? If you manage to identity them, what part of those events distorted your perspective? In other words, how did your picture of the world change? Was it positive or negative?

Ask: What coping mechanisms did I create to survive those impacting moments? How does this behavior limit your life? Do you suffer from eating disorders, compulsiveness, neurotic, or anxious behavior? Do you have additions or substance abuse problems?

Although straightforward, these questions are not readily answered: Just like exercise, begin a little at a time. Don't expect to solve all your woes with one or two tries. If you need to, write your thoughts into a journal. This can help with perspective. Integrating the above disciplines *for life* will cause you to become conscious with every thought, intention, and action. But you must be utterly honest, which can be quite painful. That is why a quiet, perhaps isolated, place is helpful when investigating your feelings. If it's too much to endure in one sitting, temporarily shelve that topic. The discipline of thoughtful reflection should become a friend—not an enemy—so do what you must to keep yourself as comfortable as possible.

Thoughtful reflection is helpful during both turbulent times, as well as, good times. Don't wait for upheavals to reflect. In happy times, our mindset is stronger and gently can pad the difficult reflection. We also feel less vulnerable and can be more accepting of those aspects that aren't particularly flattering about us. During tranquil moments, our tendency is to be more honest, and therefore, denial can dissipate. When not in the middle of deep crisis, we are less defensive and more open to new ideas. Practicing personal growth during happier moments, when all is well, freely identifies our discomfort, and reinforces that skill, so that it can be utilized during moments of stress—automatically. Our observations will always be more honest when we are feeling better. It is far more difficult to admit and recognize our responsibility while in pain and crisis.

When you discover the sources of your behavior, you have allowed the doors of change to open. Chaos ceases, and tranquility enters your reality to eliminate preconception of any kind. Single-handedly, you have tapped into the ability to heal your emotions. As you continue the path of personal growth, the result is the allowance of living in the present moment. Why does this matter? If you are busy worrying about the past or the future, and are bogged down by things you cannot change or control, you paralyze yourself from experiencing and living a moment to its fullest. In the present, all that happens is experienced completely, without judgment or expectation. Through thoughtful reflection, you understand and target the cause of bad attitudes and poor self-concepts. This process frees you to change to a positive mindset. Your "head" now has the space to harbor thoughts of your choosing. This freedom allows for a more positive and authentic you, a more flexible and spontaneous you—to enact positive solutions and changes in your life.

Personal growth frees you to change and enter into an energy field with no limitations, and all possibilities. You become mentally balanced and flexible in selecting more than one type of reaction. Choices become conscious, not unconscious, with an ability to control impulses and impulsive behavior. Emotions are stronger and deeper, and they possess clarity and definitiveness. You begin to have a special richness in experience. You will master the discipline of knowing how each feeling originates, develops, and changes, and how you are in control of it all. The ability to shift consciousness awaits you, along with ability to create a positive mindset.

Spiritual development, which is covered in the next chapter, is the third component that requires balancing. Spiritual energy promotes the attainment of worthwhile goals. It works hand in hand with all three components because it uncovers your true potential, and allows the access to inner wisdom. That knowledge creates self-fulfillment and self-reliance, and eliminates the consideration of sacrificing your goals for others. Choosing not to sacrifice your goals should not correlate to being selfish or self-centered. It is an experience of honoring who you are. People who love you will never ask you to sacrifice who you are (that's part of respect), unless of course, fear and insecurities riddle that relationship. It's all about fulfilling your human potential, and **being the best you can possibly be—for you and others**, while maintaining balance in all three components of body, mind and spirit.

When not practicing the process of thoughtful reflection, you may want to address a simple question that can be asked throughout the day. **Are my thoughts, intentions, and actions based on FEAR or LOVE?** Let's define fear and love. Most of us define fear by when we are scared out of our wits, and when we are being threatened with danger. Fear also can be worry, panic, confusion, trepidation, or apprehension, regardless of how small. It also can be worry, anxiety, or panic about any given situation—real or perceived. **Fear prevents the consideration and exploration of discomfort, as well as its solution**. You become paralyzed and accustomed to shutting down (always a fear-based reaction), which automatically puts you into a negative response. Fear is counter-productive and self-defeating, making you feel powerless. Fear imposes a preoccupation of perceived negative events and leaves us with significant energy shortages that produce stress, fatigue, and helplessness. Personal growth helps rid enough of that fear to consider and promote positive changes. We must become conscious in order to raise our awareness of fear and its power to rule our thinking.

Fear is a lack of trust. When we worry, are anxious, or panicked about upcoming events, we are mangled in self-doubt. We are preoccupied with what may or may not happen. Worry is when we don't know everything that will occur and are desperate to control an outcome, which of course, is impossible to ascertain. We are afraid that we may not attain what we want, and worse, feel unworthy of it. However, the residual panic or anxiety equates to feelings of doubt that *OUR* expectation of what should be, will not happen. Too much evaluation of an outcome also brings on paralyzing confusion, and keeps us from what we truly desire.

What is love? Love is everything that is good—and feels good. It inspires all positive reactions—trust, kindness, generosity, compassion, forgiveness, tolerance, hope, and faith. If every thought, intention, and action stemmed from the feeling of love, there would be a gentle reminder of what is good within all of us. Remembering what is good about us promotes hope, rather than despair. No negative impulses or energy would be attracted to you—and you would not engage with negativity. Love would be foremost on your mind, and negative energy—no matter how it manifests—would not be able to penetrate someone who is positive.

Next time you are angry, resentful, or disappointed, will you choose to communicate, and will you communicate through love or fear? Although angry, will you exercise control and be kind? Although resentful, will you remain flexible and loving? If disappointed, will you forgive and keep your heart open?

Sometimes, the process of personal growth can feel like we are swimming in a swamp, so resist the lure of self-pity. We all have moments that drag us down, and we all suffer from personal crises. Also, at one time or another, we have displayed dysfunctional behavior. Personal growth is about self-improvement, the kind of **improvement that leads to emotional resolutions**. We want to investigate and discard negative emotions, and unveil the best of our strengths. When our strengths and qualities have a chance to surface, (instead of our discomforts), our focus and belief turns positive. We feel better. Feeling better allows our attention to shift out of the negative—and into a world where our qualities begin to dictate the results we seek.

STRESS MANAGEMENT

Fear-based emotions cause confusion, impulsivity, depression, and anxiety—and they all lead to stress. Stress is toxic to the mind, body and spirit, and affects all three simultaneously, eventually spilling over into our relationships. Stress causes negative impact on mental function including memory loss, and physical stress such as chronic pain and illness. Negative thoughts, which stem from bad attitudes and emotional habits, poor self-concepts and self-imposed limitations, cause hoards of stress. All of that negativity translates into negative bio-chemical reactions in your body.

When it comes to the impact of on your body and mind, bio-chemical reactions can be positive or negative. For instance, stress produces unhealthy amounts of cortisol, a chemical that goes into the brain and begins to compromise brain cells—so much so, that it can begin to kill them off. Recent studies have determined a link between stress and the production of too much cortisol, to age related memory loss and Alzheimer's. Have you ever had those days when you feel very much stressed and you become forgetful, misplacing your keys, forgetting ordinary details, or outright forgetting appointments or obligations? That's too much cortisol weakening your brain function to create temporary memory loss. If this continues, you will be at risk for permanent damage to your brain. Depression also creates unhealthy chemical reactions in your body. If your state of mind continually is negative, the production of those chemicals increase to such proportions that we no longer have control. We then need to seek formalized therapy in combination with medication. These are just some of the reasons why personal growth is crucial in addressing and alleviating stress. It is an ongoing process that effectively improves our outlook in life, and therefore, our decisions.

On the positive side of bio-chemical reactions, exercise will fill our brain with endorphins and put us into better moods. Laughing and smiling can improve our health, as well as taking on tasks that are more creative—such as painting, singing, or playing an instrument. Regardless of our ability, the mere integration of these practices will strengthen and improve brain function. Dr. Eric R. Braverman, author of *The Edge Effect*, writes how these activities produce gamma amino butyric acid, which produces a calming effect, and can adjust and augment the brain's capability. He further cites that proper brain nourishment can have a dramatic impact on the quality of our lives, including the reversal or prevention of the debilitating effects of aging.

As human beings, we are resilient. Much time can pass while under high stress levels before its nasty effect manifests as an illness. Do not wait for that moment, or be arrogant enough to think that it won't affect you. With that type of thinking, the odds are not on our side. Stress creates overall energy shortages, and is detrimental to your mental and body health. All of the above should make us care.

Fear of any kind escalates stress. Panic attacks, high anxiety, freak-outs, hostility, and violence, all stem from too much stress. Also, being around people who behave like that induces stress. Do you limit those interactions? When it comes to the type of people with whom you choose to spend time, are you selective? Do you pay particular attention to whether or not they support or drag you down? People cause stress. Do you excuse family members or close friends who refuse to control their outbursts, rages, and other extreme reactions as, "Well, that's just the way they are?" Oftentimes, we tend to pool personality with behavior. Many of us allow those types of people to behave that way so that we don't "rock the boat." We claim that there is nothing we can do. Why? It's easier not to deal with our own fear of confrontation, reprisal, or judgment. That type of thinking not only invites that type of person and behavior to us, but also begins its permanent etching into our cells as negativity, thus inducing stress and draining our energy.

Every time you react out of fear rather than love, stress creeps up to attack you. Bad relationships, jobs, and environments cause stress. Loud noise, deadlines and over-booked schedules—all cause stress. Where will you draw the line and make choices that lead to positive change? What will be your stress reducing activities? Is your overall health and balance important enough to integrate those activities, or are you still busy holding up a social mask showing what you want people to believe, rather than showing them who you really are?

Like it or not, excuse or no excuse, this is the moment when you will have to make a very important decision. **Will I honor or dishonor myself?** Will I care enough about myself to make the positive changes I know I should—or continue saying that I can't? There's no room for postponement if you are to contribute the best of what you can be to yourself and others—especially if you are raising children, who are looking to you as an example. Do I respect, admire, and love myself enough to do what's best for me, in order to do what's best for others? Will I be dedicated to alleviating my stress level, or will I insist that I simply don't have enough time? Which will it be?

It is imperative not to stress yourself while doing positive things that turn negative because you don't use your internal compass. That compass called your life IQ, guides and dictates when enough is enough.

For example, perhaps you've just had one of the most difficult days in the office, or you're a mom who ran around all day ˉdriving your kids to school, their activities and play dates, besides dealing with the uncooperative cable guy and nasty cashier at the supermarket. Rather than coming home and kicking your feet up, and perhaps having a cool refreshment, you insist on doing that exercise routine you just implemented last week. You are on a mission to lose those inches and pounds. Despite outright fatigue, you still exercise. You exhaust yourself even more, so much so that your body becomes over-stimulated and stressed—and later, that night's sleep is compromised. The next day starts off with even more fatigue and stress that perpetuates a vicious cycle of stressful events. Let's all take a deep breath. **What all of this means is that we need to avoid excessive exercise, dieting, self-analysis, and all stress-inducing activities.**

No need to bury your head in your lap thinking all is hopeless. We all are experiencing similar stresses. There are things that you can do to alleviate stress. Coping skills are important to develop when managing stress levels, and chances are, you have already developed a few. Social support generally is easy to find, and includes friends and partners who allow you to talk through your problems and concerns. If you have no one to talk to, you will have to make friends. Being a loner in life is impractical and goes against the inherent nature of human beings; we are social creatures requiring interaction. Perhaps there is a coworker you trust, perhaps there is a person you see every day at the coffee shop. Maybe you can find an interest and join a group that enjoys the same. Strike up some conversation. Sometimes that's all we need to do to know that we aren't really alone, and aren't the only ones feeling like we're losing control.

What do you do to relax? It's called leisure time. Do you have any? This is your moment to do something for yourself. Just like with personal growth, we need to focus and find emotional releases; otherwise unresolved emotions could turn into hostility, rage, and other intense, reactive behavior. Exercise and physical activity of any kind are great stress reducing activities. Do something that makes you *feel* good, provided it does not hurt you or others. Run a mile, eat a pastry, get a facial, or call a friend. Read a book, watch a movie, or cook an exotic meal. Any time dedicated to leisure time decreases emotional wear and tear on our body and our mind.

If you have embarked on the road to personal growth, and have been working on bad, learned behavior, you will decrease stress. No more negative responses to worry about—and your reactions have changed to the positive, particularly during difficult moments. Perhaps you are integrating the process of mind over matter. This exercise can be the simple uttering of words, a refusal to allow negativity to affect you. *And* you do it no matter what happens. Do you ever notice those people who are in total control of their reactions while all hell breaks loose? It's mind over matter, and not some extraordinary ability to be affected less than you. **It is a conscious choice to be the best they can be—even in circumstances that seem dire**.

MIND MAINTENANCE

Unleashing a healthy and powerful mind

This is where how you care for your body starts paying off. Nutrition, supplements, and exercise, positively fuel the mind. A healthy mind and body boosts immunity. If they are not in balance, decision-making will be compromised. When you are stressed, whether through environment or because you over-or-under eat, or haven't yet embarked on a path to personal growth—you short-circuit yourself by depleting energy to your mind. Your mind becomes cloudy and forgetful, and harbors negativity to affect the quality of your life experiences. You will become unable to unleash your true potential, and you will feel like a prisoner throughout your lifetime. On the other hand, if you respect your body and mind, fueling it with nutrition, rest, and exercise, blood flow will increase to the brain. This will encourage optimal mental fitness, and will improve memory, mood, and concentration. Good body and mind habits ensure a good metabolism that equips you with the ability to promote regeneration and resurgence of energy. If you successfully break your problematic conditioning, your life slate is wiped clean—thus, putting you into the amazing place of all possibilities.

ENERGY MINUS vs. ENERGY PLUS

While on the road to improving your life IQ for body-mind-spirit balance, there are exercises you can do that are outright proactive and instantaneous with results. Simply, eliminate energy minuses and incorporate energy pluses.

Examples of Energy Minus

Begin by putting a stop to complaining and criticizing. Ever hear the saying, "If you have nothing good to say, say nothing at all"? It is always easier to find something wrong, than to find something right. Some of our hyper-inflated realities, like not finding the right dress for a party, or owning a European sports car, stem from a society that is rich and spoiled. Let's face it, most of us in the United States are spoiled, compared to other people who suffer with poverty or terminal illness, or both. We have it so good that "complaining" has become a national pastime. Do you ever listen to strangers' conversation in beauty salons, restaurants, airports, or doctor's waiting rooms? People are concerned about insignificant things, which initially can be overlooked—until neuroses creep up to incapacitate your existence. Complaining will exacerbate other problems. You may lose friends because no one likes to hang around someone who continually is dissatisfied. Also, the dissatisfaction you project will end up attracting exactly the same type of people to you. Even if you do have real crises and concerns, it's better to direct that energy and effort searching for positive solutions. **Try being grateful and appreciating what you have, not what you don't have.** Also, be careful when criticizing becomes chronic. This activity quickly exposes a person's insecurities. People who put down others and their ideas, are projecting THEIR own dissatisfaction in life. It's always easier to put down what someone else is doing, when you are not happy with your life.

Stop making assumptions as to what others are doing, let alone thinking. Too many of us are spending time imagining that we know what others are thinking and feeling, as well as what motivates those people to be the way that they are. This unproductive activity of preoccupation translates into unnecessary worry, concern, and anxiety about things over which you truly have no control. First, those things are imagined, and second, they are most likely negative. Negative preoccupation induces high doses of stress. Why do you care anyway, and what makes you think that you know? Does your day really improve because you think you have figured out the negative reasoning behind someone's actions, let alone thoughts? You are not in anyone's head, so stay inside your own. Your only responsibility is to your own thoughts, intentions, and actions. Presuming that somehow you know the thoughts, intentions, and actions of others, only drains precious energy. If what you think and do is positive and out of love, there is nothing with which to be concerned. However, if you are suspicious, scheming, and anticipatory of only bad things to come, they shall indeed—and so will the people who instigate that sort of behavior and negativity. If you are making chronic assumptions about what other people are thinking and feeling, it is a strong indicator that you have negative, unresolved feelings from your past. Listen very carefully to what you are accusing someone else of thinking or feeling—those accusations generally refer to the way you feel about yourself. The same holds true for the positive. If you keep yourself busy thinking about all that is good, particularly about people and their actions, you will attract all that is good. More will follow about this in the chapter of *Spirit*. There is a better way to find out what people are thinking and feeling: ASK!

Get away from labels and categories—in what you do, and how you think. This activity is someone else's idea of what's acceptable and what isn't. We all have a mind that functions on its own, so let's use it! Don't behave like a child who needs guidance and approval for acceptance. Isn't the world diverse enough to suit your particular need or desire without having to mold yourself into the "correct" label or category? Do you rely on others completely, relinquishing any and all responsibility to yourself and your actions? **Think for yourself!** Thinking is part of an active and healthy mind that doesn't fear to express good thoughts and ideas. Remember, you don't need to be *right* in order to express a thought. When it comes to living, being right is subjective—and all about feeding a starving ego. No matter who they are, no one person has the correct idea.

If you drop the labels, the pressure will come off *immediately*. You no longer will care if what you wear, how you think, or what you feel is appropriate. This process brings you closer and closer to your essence—the essence of who you really are—without discomfort. It's an easier way to live because it relinquishes unnecessary social stress, and allows for the even flow of energy.

Fight the urge to listen to others when your internal guide begins to hammer away. It's the moment when someone insists that you feel one way, while everything inside of you rejects that advice. No matter how well-intentioned that person or advice is, don't ignore your internal compass when it guides you in the opposite direction. Instead, tune in and listen to your natural advisor. It never will steer you wrong because all the while, you will be tuned into yourself. Thus, whatever you do, will be right for you. Even mistakes, if decided on our own, become productive. They build resilience to help us through to the next hurdle. Our decisions, triumphs, and mistakes are best for us and easier to live with, unlike someone else's. But you're not alone. We all seek out comfort while in the midst of problem solving. We all hope that the answers are easy, waiting on a silver platter. Don't kid yourself, and pay attention to your internal director.

Stop making excuses when the real truth is that you cannot admit that you are unwilling to change and make a decision. Thinking and re-thinking, and citing external elements as the reason for not doing something, wastes far too much energy. For instance, you may be thinking of moving to a new city or town because you feel the opportunities for you have dried up. However, you've been talking about it for years. You cite all sorts of reasons—not enough money, can't find the right apartment, not sure if you will like the people in that town, and so forth. Maybe, you continually are making excuses why you haven't left the relationship that you claim makes you unhappy. You continue to say that it's not the right time and/or you don't want to hurt your partner. Perhaps, you've been talking about writing the great American novel, and you've barely written a chapter. Rather than acknowledging to yourself that you may not be ready to make that decision—or don't want to—you engage in negative mental wrestling.

Wouldn't it be more productive to just shift gears into the positive and better utilize that energy for solutions or better things to do? Stop talking about things that you are unprepared to do. If you're not going to do them, then don't do them. And if you are ready, DO IT! Choose to do it, or not to do it, change, or don't change—drop the excuses. This activity induces stress by further discouraging you, and it becomes tiresome for those that are within hearing range of those excuses.

Regarding the aforementioned topic of shifting gears, we must address one major reality of the Twenty-first Century—*time*. How often have we heard ourselves say, "I don't have the time?" Here's the simple definition of this overused excuse. This is double talk for "I don't want to make the effort required to make that change, or changes right now." Get real. We all have time constraints in our lives, but when we decide that something is a priority, we manage to squeeze it in.

There is another type of excuse that must be eliminated when making choices. **Do not justify your bad actions by making excuses**. For instance, because your relationship is suffering with some unresolved issues, you might choose to have an affair and justify it by blaming your partner's inequities, lack of attention, or blatant disregard of your feelings. Stop the pretense. Your job is to address your feelings with your partner, stay or get out of that relationship, but *not* to choose bad behavior sprinkled with excuses.

One last note, try to cut down on how much news you absorb, whether through television or the Internet. Too much news is a source of stress; rarely is it positive, and it keeps us over-stimulated. Visual media is the worst proponent when it comes to high stress pictures, sounds and lighting. They purposefully are exaggerated to capture our attention.

Examples of Energy Plus

Focus on a solution and detach from the problem. The problem still will be there, but the difference will be that it won't muddle your thinking when a time of crisis requires a clear head. Shift out of negative and into positive. Search for solutions rather than indulging in self-pity. Whatever choices you make, and the better tuned in you are to your internal compass, the closer you will get to the best choices for you. The more you think and focus on solutions, the more possibilities will arise. Find that silver lining and know that one exists— no matter what the circumstance.

Be positive, even outrageously positive in everything. Don't be afraid to think big when it comes to all things positive. Except for death, nothing is the end of the world. A positive solution exists! So, go and find it!

Be conscious with your thoughts, intentions, and actions. Utilize a conscious effort to put your best foot forward. Consciously behave with a positive mindset, and while you're walking down the path of life, **be aware of others, and treat everyone the way you want to be treated!** That way, you are able to appreciate the wonder of each experience, while bringing a positive awareness of what moves you and others. If you're negative in your thoughts, intentions, and actions, the extraordinary moments in life definitely will pass you by.

Live only in the present. Our past and future is the next thing holding us back after fear. Live in the present, but understand your past to know its impact on your future.

Make friends of all age groups. It helps with perspective and expands your thinking past your own version of reality.

Keep a fertile mind! Learn and do new things. If you have finished your formal education, or have none at all, keep learning—and learn from others! New information challenges your mind, and keeps it active. If learning slows, so does the mind. In order for your brain to function, you need to use it. Simple tasks do count, such as playing games, writing, painting, reading, conversing, and exchanging ideas; it all keeps the dendrites connecting—in a way, exercising, to remain healthy and strong.

Find a worthwhile goal, if you don't have one. This might very well mean what you do for a living, or the many hobbies you might pursue. Find something you are passionate about. If you don't know what to do, try to volunteer and help those in need. This promotes personal growth and learning, instead of stagnation. Helping others keeps the focus off of you and your problems, and broadens perspective. Any worthwhile goal will help when those difficult moments in life arise. You readily will manage those times better by "holding" on to your worthwhile goal, despite what's not working in your life. This then will push you in the direction of achieving your highest potential—a place where you can feel fulfilled, and a place for which you are destined.

LAUGH and smile every day. Don't take yourself or life so seriously. A strong mind can carry you forward when your body is weak. Laugh at yourself and your setbacks. It's the purest of revenge during moments of crises.

MEDITATE – Many of us have looked upon meditation as something strange, "guru"-like and certainly, not "of" the West. In fact, the practice of formalized meditation does stem from the East, but guess what? In a less formalized way, you already have been doing it. Meditation is thought, deliberation, consideration, contemplation, and/or reflection. You have been doing it with the practice of personal growth. However, if we desire further exploration, formalized meditation may be exactly what you need. Meditation can be difficult, but only because you have not yet trained your mind to turn off the noise in our head. It does take patience. We encourage the investigation and practice of meditation, but regardless of your personal interest, consider the following practice:

Try integrating the following discipline during moments of high stress, panic, or anxiety. It is based on the standard yogic practice of breathing 4-7-8, and it was introduced by Dr. Andrew Weil many years ago. This breathing exercise is a simple way to relieve stress and improve blood flow, thus slowing blood pressure. Breathing 4-7-8 also calms and soothes our respiration. 4-7-8 refers to the counting of seconds while you inhale or exhale breath. To accurately count a second, follow each number by saying "thousand" - one thousand, two thousand, three thousand, and so forth. Begin by sitting up straight and inhaling air as deeply as possible for four seconds. Force the breath to expand your diaphragm. Feel your ribcage expand. Hold it for seven seconds (which could be difficult), then release for eight seconds, pushing all of the air out of you. You will find that eight seconds can be a long time, so exhale loudly until each second is mentally uttered!

After three or four tries of breathing 4-7-8, you will feel rejuvenated, and if interested in meditating, you will be ready to focus on your breath and the sound of your breathing. It has a calming effect, which then invites the challenge of clearing your mind of the internal dialogue, turbulence of negativity, and stress-related thinking. Know that the process of meditating into the calm can take many tries. We all have been programmed into a high-stress lifestyle that prevents the calming of our mind. Be patient when practicing the art of meditation.

Finally, bring things of beauty and pleasure into your surroundings. Spend time with nature. Appease your senses. Bring into your life flowers, music, food, and people—anything that lifts your spirit!

V.

SPIRIT

Spirit is the birthplace of your internal compass, the essence of who you really are. The idiosyncratic composition of your individuality—the abilities, talents, goals and dreams—the essential qualities that make you distinct from all others—rests within your spirit. This part of you inextricably is linked to the body and the mind. Like the mind, spirit is not material, but is a powerful source of energy. Our spirit—our soul—has specific advantages. It is vibrant and intuitive, alive and creative. It is strong, sure, and resilient. Spirit is so strong a life force that it can manifest as your "will" to live. If we dissect that cliché, in the instance when nothing else works to save our life, our will has the power to keep us living. That "will" gives us the strength to survive, persevere, and succeed—and it can steam-roll over any perceived obstacle. Spirit is the highest source of energy that fuels our existence.

When we nurture this extraordinary component, we produce a strong, healthy, and aware spirit. We develop the ability to trigger all opportunities and possibilities. This awareness provides the faith necessary to take plans and desires forward. Spirit inspires unadulterated ideas, imagination, and is a steady, lifelong source of direction. There is no stagnation, confusion, or fear. You are left with the ability and belief that you can attain and achieve anything. Developing and practicing spirituality unravels a strong spirit that in turn, creates a stronger body and mind—directing positive energy and results. This intangible energy weathers storms, and attracts what is needed to achieve your goals throughout your lifetime.

Ancient Greeks (first documented by Galen, a Greek medical doctor and philosopher ca 130–ca 210 AD) believed that the essence of the human soul (spirit) was located in the pineal gland, a pea-sized organ located in the middle of the brain. Known as the "third eye," this intuitive center began its referencing to those particularly gifted with strong intuitive ability and clairvoyance, and historically has maintained respect and reverence amongst many—from ancient to modern day cultures. Renée Descartes (French philosopher and mathematician) further documented the essence of the pineal gland, and in 1888, Helena Petrovna Blavatsky, founder of the Theosophical Society, reaffirmed the belief of spiritual connection, citing the pineal gland as the "eye of Shiva" of the Hindu mystics and as the organ to spiritual vision.

By the late 1950s, research validated this tiny organ as the intuitive and cognitive reasoning center. Scientists uncovered that the chemical secretions of the pineal gland help to instill individuality and creativity, regulate and provide euphoric emotions, relieve stress and anxiety, and are responsible for inter-dimensional spiritual connections. Further, physicists successfully have measured the energy of our spirit upon death to weigh twenty-one grams. When we die, the energy of our spirit is released into the atmosphere, clearly expending that energy into another world, one that is not material. What is that world, and how might we communicate with that world? It's up for debate, but scientists busily have been trying to disprove the existence of an afterlife. Thus far, they have been unsuccessful. However, for our purposes, this information is meant to validate that as human beings, we possess the power of spirit—but generally abandon the exercise of the single most important component of our existence, leaving its potential entirely up to chance.

With all of that ability within our spirit, imagine what happens when stress enters our system to retard its normal function. We don't sleep, lack creativity, experience limited emotions, individuality wanes, and hopelessness develops. It infects our entire body-mind system. When we are physically sick, there is an exterior and obvious illness to address. When sick in our spirit, it is internal, and despite success in other areas of our lives, we continue to suffer, or feel dissatisfied and lost. If the "will" dies, despite our perceived physical and mental fitness, we die. **Spirit is our life force and it is strengthened by spiritual development.**

First, we must adjust the true meaning of spirit and spirituality. Spirituality is *NOT* religion, New Age, or any organized institution created by mankind. Religion is cultural, which is why many different religions exist. Its rules and regulations merely reflect a society's desire for spiritual and moral leadership, as well as defining and interpreting its concepts. Culture and tradition can be beautifully depicted through religion and its teachings. History, folklore, and rituals are intertwined to foster a meaningful life. Just like laws, religion is meant to harness, connect, and create a sense of order. Understandably, society has made religion synonymous with spirituality, as if to say, that if you are spiritual, you are religious; if you're not religious but spiritual, you are "New Age" or some other group by default. Not so.

These organized institutions have persuaded many of us into believing that they monopolize the interpretation of spirit and spirituality. They also have discouraged many, who for one reason or another, cannot abide by the types of rules and requirements to meet acceptance, therefore ostracizing many who wish to develop their spirit. As a result, society has become more secular—an attitude that can be helpful by not discriminating against those who practice religion—but at the same time, an attitude also can develop that has encouraged a lack of regard toward spiritual energy, and the practice of spirituality.

Since ancient times, spirituality long has been the interpretation of mysticism, first through the forces of nature, then by the delineation of gods interpreted by high priests, tribal leaders, and mystics. Religious leaders and philosophers followed, by integrating dogma to mysticism, and have been preaching their point of view for thousands of years. It is understandable how some of us have come to know spirituality as the study of religion, when in fact it is the study of mysticism. However, it is important to note that Eastern and Western religious leaders and philosophers long have studied mysticism, and we rely on their teachings as a foundation to spiritual practice. Also, knowingly or unknowingly, we are ruled by spiritual laws. There are many, and they have been deeply woven into our society. For instance, spiritual laws include that of Success (or Abundance), Tolerance, Responsibility, Integrity, Forgiveness, Service and Compassion. The list is lengthy, and worth exploring. However, this information is a basis for understanding that these laws exist to explain human nature, and have been analyzed to formulate the rules we accept in society.

Erase the notion that spirituality = religion, New Age, or any organized cult—or that religion, New Age, or any organized cult = spirituality. Instead, we will be including spirit as a final component of energy that contributes to our state of well-being in body, and in mind. The process of spirituality is entirely up to us, and its practice should be determined by us as well. However, it is important to emphasize that if religion, New Age, or another group, or the entirety of nature is your special way of accessing the inner self and its relationship with all that is around us, including a God, utilize that belief as you so choose. Be aware that there are many ways of accessing spirit, and being spiritual. We are interested in developing balance, and *exercising* your spirit as a necessary component to improving your life IQ.

Our mere existence defines us with a spirit, and therefore, we are spiritual beings. The spirit displays multiple characteristics, but there are three that are dominant. First, our spirit is our soul. Our spirit is our inner self, our essence, our individuality. It is our inner wisdom, and is there, no matter how little or how much we utilize it. The second characteristic is the strength of that spirit. Strength of spirit is projected through integrity. It is the level of courage and moral fiber we adhere to in order to be honest, truthful, and reliable— particularly to ourselves. The third aspect to our spirit is the ability to reflect all that we are feeling. It manifests as an attitude, mood, tendency, or atmosphere of who we truly are. **If we live aligned with our spirit, our life is that of honor and vitality. We live the deepest and truest nature of who we are.**

Since we are spiritual beings, let's define what that entails. It means that we are divine and heavenly. As spirit, we are virtuous and flawless—sacred and blessed. We are honorable and committed. Imagine. All of us are defined with such greatness and potential—it cannot be more powerful than that, yet so many have allowed their spirit to rest dormant and underutilized, unable to access our inherent birthright to experience life with meaning. Spiritually, we are equal, and we are validated by that description. **When**

we do not develop spiritually, we are disconnected from this flawless divinity. This—and only this—is the reason why material realities are insufficient when on the quest to attain success in all aspects of our life.

Without a commitment to spiritual development, one leg in the chair of successful living continually will malfunction. Energy will be compensated to make up for that malfunction, and energy shortages will exist. Although you may think that all is relatively stable in your life, do you ever feel like you lack passion or creativity? Or, in your search for more direction, you lack solutions, and you assume that there's nothing you can do because you've tried everything? Do you aimlessly wrestle with options, and feel like there's nothing but quicksand beneath you? Perhaps you are anxious and preoccupied, unable to find a sense of calm. This is called being *out of touch* with spirit. We will uncover how to develop spirit into our highest potential as human beings. We will develop the life force that craves passion, imagination, intuitiveness, and creativity. Coupled with our commitment to personal growth, when we silence our internal dialogue, freeing it from bad emotional habits and poor self-concepts, we begin to access spirit. Spiritual development begins to control negative, mental urges, and that action will summon the energy of spirit.

Whether drudgery, curiosity, or the onset of some horrific circumstance or experience pushes us into the consideration of spiritual development, a leap of *faith* most definitely is required. When it comes to our spirit, there is nothing to hold onto but thin air, so let's try to give it a little more substance. **Spirit is the platform of the mind.** It enhances the abilities of the mind, and fine tunes our thoughts and feelings. Spiritual development is a type of higher learning—learning to understand that we are able to become better, do better and strive for better. Spirit expands those thoughts and feelings far beyond normal limitations. In fact, they have no limitations. When we develop spiritually, we tap into our individuality, which is like no one else's. We release the limitations of the physical world to *see* ourselves clearly. This is a kind of sacred contract we have with ourselves to be the best we can be in life—to become all that we are capable of becoming. Who we can become nurtures faith. That faith in the self leads us to our rightful path, one that creates a sense of peace and acceptance in our lives. **Spirit inspires us out of mediocrity, and brings fulfillment and purpose**. Accessing spirit begins with the mind that consciously shifts into slowing down—enough to enter the calm of our spirit. Our spirit then directs and guides us to our natural abilities, and allows us to create our dreams. It makes us think about how we can expand, and it guides us throughout our lifetime. Know that the choice to become acquainted with the higher self is what leads us directly into our haven of inner wisdom.

POWER OF CONDITIONING vs. POWER OF SPIRIT

Conditioning can suffocate the spirit and will breed weakness, uncertainty, and fear. When you do not maintain spiritual practice, your tendency is to rely on external information, and you are prone to being influenced by outside factors, including the thinking of others. The unfamiliar territory of deciding what to do with your life, regardless of your age, becomes a troubling expedition. We want answers. If we develop spiritually, we begin to have remarkable faith in what we believe we would like to achieve—even if initially, we have no idea of how that's going to get done. Spirit breeds love and all of its positive emotional offshoots, such as courage, which is required when we tackle the unknown—what life really is. On the other hand, conditioning, (what you believe externally), can disassemble who you truly are by imposing the type of thinking that precludes you from contributing the best of you. It's the type of thinking from others that insists that you don't have what it takes to become what you want, or the self-imposed thinking of defeat prior to doing anything. This includes getting preoccupied with worrying too much about how others will judge you. As mentioned in the chapter of *Beliefs & Conditioning,* we ascertained that conditioning imposes the type of thinking that we should only accept and be comfortable with the norm. It is a process that makes us believe that we will not have a choice should we disagree with that standard. As adults, we are reminded what education and jobs will be right for us, what and who will make us happy, and how material wealth will validate our existence. Is it a wonder we grow up into adults continually questioning who we are and what we really want—everything from the people we choose to be with, to the types of lives we are living?

However, when you trust spirit, you develop faith in what you believe is right for you. You begin to trust that what you want is doable, what you believe is possible, despite the odds, and despite the people who are busy trying to convince you otherwise. The power of spirit enables you to attain exactly what you want, in a way where you no longer feel pressure, discomfort or threat, in pursuing what you truly desire. When you access spirit, you do not feel threatened by or afraid of anything or anyone—and if you are, you are prepared to fight with the wisdom and courage of spirit.

LIMITATION vs. EXPANSION

In the physical world, no matter what it is, there is always a beginning and an end. It then would follow that there are limits on what can be done in the physical world. **Spiritually, there are no limitations**. Spiritual power rests inside each of us, and when accessed, allows us to imagine bigger and greater things. It allows for that one doctor to imagine a cure, or an architect to imagine a building like no other. It allows an athlete to imagine the breaking of records, and the ordinary person to imagine the fame of a superstar. Spirit allowed for the imagination of the airplane, telephone, computer and space travel. Anything or anyone imposing limits on how broad things are, in other words, how they are finite, is limited by definition. History continues to demonstrate that "thinking" perpetually is evolving throughout time. Barriers are broken, concepts are expanded, and change is undertaken. **Finite thinking equates to conditioning**, and again, we need to ask, "What is conditioning, and what is not", when it comes to how we truly feel.

When we connect with our spiritual energy, we enter a world of endless expansion. The spirit becomes the most influential energy source—it has no limitations, so it trumps the energy sources of the body and the mind. However, when you utilize the entire energy field of body, mind and spirit, the expression is dynamic. That type of energy infuses a perspective that absolutely everything is possible. Our spirit gives us the strength to blind ourselves to all perceived obstacles. It doesn't mean that we no longer see obstacles, but we do learn to treat obstacles as part of the plan. As a result, enthusiasm flourishes, and we are no longer distracted by negative perceptions. **Spirit provides the belief and staying power necessary for us to do all things extraordinary**.

Many of us have been making positive improvements with our body and/or mind, and have done little—or nothing—to develop spiritually. The result of this oversight is a malfunction in your equilibrium. Unconsciously, you will compensate your energy to make up for that malfunction, and energy shortages will continue to exist. These energy shortages will appear as dissatisfaction, emptiness, or confusion—even if you have evaluated what you consider to be your issues. These lingering feelings may not be blatant, but your search for more meaning will persist, and will continue to tug at your energy. You will not operate optimally, and the quality of your life will be compromised. That doesn't mean that your life will appear to be externally inadequate, but it does mean you will not operate at your highest potential, thus limiting the possibilities and opportunities in every aspect of your life. *That* drains energy. Our goal is to uncover the power of spirit, and find our balance, so that we can develop our purest potential.

THE PRACTICALITY OF SPIRITUAL DEVELOPMENT

We must begin by acknowledging the existence of spirit, and accepting that we are spiritual beings. If you don't feel anything different, just learn to trust that spirit is there. Start by **considering your spirit a priority**. Then, consider that we are spiritual beings first, and physical beings second. Why? When we see ourselves as physical first, our entire reality is one of limitations, and the limitations that exist in a physical world. It's an obvious next step to think this way because in the physical sense and definition, we all have physical limitations, including that of death. *That* limits our thinking, which in turn, limits our spirit. If we don't see ourselves as spirit, our perspectives continually focus on the limits of the physical world, thus limiting us, and our rightful road to meaningful living.

Know that biology (our physical body) merely is the representative of who we are—the reflection. It takes spirit to unleash potential—and we are naturally drawn to it. Do you ever notice those people who, regardless of their physical exterior, exude so much positive energy that their beauty manifests into an air of being alive, exuberant, and "together?" *And* no matter what or how, we want to be a part of it? Inside ourselves, we all have that vitality. In all that we do, our spirit distinguishes us with the entirety of our decision-making. It is our personal signature that can create remarkable achievements and lead us toward the highest quality of living. If our choices are not really ours, but someone else's idea of choices, our spirit rests dormant within our energy field, unable to fuel our highest potential. We handcuff this life force because our spirit only awakens by our command, not someone else's.

Evaluating what we believe and making choices that truly are ours, is critical to our life experience. Dr. Bruce Lipton, author of *The Biology of Belief*, proves how emotions regulate your genetic expression—and that we are not victims of our genes. This understanding is a milestone for human evolution, and validates why we need to review our beliefs. If our thoughts—and thus, what we believe—have the power to alter our DNA, and if we harbor negative perspectives of what we can achieve, we cannot escape the prison of being a victim. The book emphasizes that instead of being constrained by society's mainstream view that we are limited by our genetics, **we can live to unleash our true spiritual potential by transforming our beliefs**. This process requires that we connect with our spiritual energy—who we truly are—so that we can live the kind of life where anything is possible.

All of us face challenges in life, but when do our choices cross over into violating who we really are? If we do not develop spiritually, we are not communicating with the part of us that desires a higher quality of living—the part of us that understands that we *can* have and do better. As mentioned in the chapter of *Mind*, our fearful beliefs distort reality, and these beliefs prevent us from attaining what we want. When fear is a part of our lives, it influences how we express ourselves and communicate with the world. Our tendency is not to trust a positive outcome of events. If we do not develop spiritually, our communication with the self is one of fear, and we halt our ability to progress.

Who we are (spirit) and what we believe (mind) are inseparable. Not knowing who we are drags us into realities that will always be lacking, confused, or uncommitted—where those nasty voices and negative internal dialogue have a chance to hammer away. Know that those are the voices that powerfully call out what you can experience in life. Those voices are there, waiting patiently as our life unfolds to present a set of circumstances as negative. These circumstances give us an opportunity to learn about ourselves. Do we learn and evaluate the illusory boundaries of fear, or do we dismiss that situation as some fluke of negativity? No matter what we choose to do, our spirit has a desire to experience the best in life, a desire to be understood, but that includes what we fear—a belief we need to overcome. We cannot attain what we want in life if we do not acknowledge our fear. Avoiding fear chokes us into depression, anxiety and physical illness.

For instance, if your esteem suffers in a way that says you are not worthy, your life will project the same. You will end up with situations where you will feel and believe that you are unworthy. Another example is when you frequently find yourself with people you cannot trust. You may have issues with trust—not because those people may or may not be trustworthy, but your suspicious ways invite those you cannot trust. What ends up happening is that who we are (spirit) becomes mixed up with fear (produced by the mind), and we create unhealthy situations, making unhealthy choices. We begin to package this fear by creating reasonable sounding needs and ideas of how life should be, and we become prisoners of those perceptions. We change who we are (our spirit) from something positive and healing—into negative misconceptions about life and who we are. *This* will make us sick, either physically or mentally, or both. **Spiritual development helps to remove fear by expanding our knowledge, wisdom, and understanding of the self.**

However, no matter where we may be in understanding spirit, this unusual energy does have a way of imposing its virtue. Do you ever experience those moments when you finally realize that your decision to do something is *so* right that it unleashes the kind of defiance against what you originally thought—in a way where you miraculously take action? Perhaps you've made the type of decision that frees you from the pressure you have been feeling for far too long? Have you ever experienced those "light bulb" moments that liberate you from limited thinking—and then suddenly, you really believe that what you wanted to do is possible? This is the experience of spiritual energy, the moments when we feel the goodness of who we are, and it is the kind of energy that positively intensifies what we want to achieve. It is the energy of change that heals us with respect, admiration, and love of the self.

Thoughtful reflection is the foremost way to access spirit. It improves our concentration, and allows us to focus on one thing only. This shift toward specific attention opens the door to the virtue of spirit. Whether we call it meditation, prayer, or thoughtful reflection, we must embrace this practice as the way to our better and higher self. If not, the blurring of the physical world interrupts our ability to access spirit. Spirit is not material, and requires patience for the surfacing of this commanding component. Understand that **patience merely is the training of the mind to detach from everyday annoyances and problems**, and is the only way to enter our inner wisdom. Calm is required to access spirit. Patience provides us with clear thinking, and the time to know ourselves. In practicing patience, we create the endurance to measure and test our ideals. When we *see* our ideals as doable, we begin to utilize faith. **Faith breeds trust.** It affords us the type of persistence to understand ourselves, to tolerate difficulties, and to consider the exploration of other advantageous possibilities. This creates a superlative platform of positive energy that fuels our entire body-mind system.

Honoring spirit means honoring ourselves. It starts with honoring our body-mind, but despite the honoring of those components, we still will experience moments when the body-mind is insufficient to maneuver our success without spirit. In our minds, we might know what we want, but the direction is one of uncertainty. This can frighten us, and since the mind is pliable, we *will* (with the power of our will) what our mind should think and believe. If we honor spirit by honoring what we truly want, spirit gives us the courage to go forward with uncertainly, and executes the changes we desire. Fear forcefully is pushed aside, and we are inspired to trust that what comes will be extraordinary.

If we honor our spirit by making the conscious decision to develop and nurture its existence, we automatically move closer to being who we really are, and not that person who hides behind façades. Let's be realistic with the journey of life. We are looking for answers, and the material world doesn't always provide the solutions. Accessing spirit means going deeper within you, in order to enter this sacred realm. It's a leap of faith into something higher and intangible. Forget about those who only believe in the here and now, and are busy intellectualizing solely through physical realities. Skeptics of any kind generally find solace in only what *they* can understand or prove, again, exposing limited thinking. When it comes to spirituality, this is another way conditioning influences our mind. Try explaining the feeling of falling in love and from where it comes, or more importantly, explaining why you believe in yourself. It is intangible; yet powerful enough to make things happen.

What happens when we honor our spirit through thoughtful reflection? We will begin to experience the evolution of insight that inspires solutions. Our own special path will unfold by the unveiling of all possibilities. This unveiling is so precise that the solutions coming up are the "aha moments" that give us the confidence to go forward. We become patient in this unraveling process, accepting that when the time is right, we automatically will be alerted to our destiny. It is like going down the road in cruise control; you know where you're going, (in this case, the road of life), but it isn't until you see a sign that you know it's time to turn off at an exit. If you take the time to listen to your spirit, forgoing the physical reality of time constraints, the answer always will be there.

How do you *hear* your spirit? When you silence your mind in a way where you empty your thoughts enough to enter a state of continued calm, inspiring thoughts will follow. It does take practice and time. Sometimes, we can believe that the thoughts that popped up were spirit, rather than our mind. How will you know the difference? You will feel a positive surge of something very *right*.

As a first step for balance in spirit, **INTEGRITY** must be integrated into your vocabulary with all that you do. Exactly what is that? **It is the type of behavior that is honest, truthful, and upright.** Behaving in any other way is dishonest and deceitful. It may not sound flattering, but we need to identify behavior for what it is. For far too long, as a society, we have accepted subtle allowances for deceitful behavior. White lies are not really lying, omissions and half-truths are the norm, and downright mean-spiritedness has permeated our value system as acceptable. Also, we casually disregard our lack of integrity by allowing powerful negative messaging. This negative messaging is reinforced by some of our societal role models, including those in authority. Politicians, musicians, people in the media, athletes, and a few in corporate America are busy selectively choosing to relinquish responsibility when it is convenient. Is it a wonder our spirit remains locked away? **It is critical to accept that integrity will begin to strengthen our spirit.**

Let's boil this back down to an individual level. Integrity strengthens our spirit because it allows us to express our authentic self. **This is the moment you decide how you will have a relationship with yourself.** Unless we are honest with ourselves, we are not able to be honest with others. HONESTY in who you are, leads to honesty in what you want, and what you do. This is a must because you can draw your spirit force into what you *think* you want. Your goal might be one that includes approval, whether from your family or friends, or you might be appeasing other insecurities.

The result will be unhappiness, a kind of haunting emptiness, despite the attainment of what you think you wanted. You ignore spirit, deny it has impact, and continue with *that* acceptable decision.

For instance, you want a bigger house, or new car, to keep up with that new community you just moved into. You attain it, yet you still feel as empty as ever. It's acceptable to want beautiful material things—they are some of the physical rewards in life. But, you're heading for trouble when your decision is laced with the desire to impress others, fit-in, or other insecurities that might plague you. Material rewards are temporary, and no matter what, will NEVER fill in the emptiness that is calling out for you to change.

Don't exclude yourself from the aforementioned because you are materially wealthy. You may no longer desire material wealth, but the demon of power definitely will chase you. What does this mean? Simply, you will be tempted to control situations and people with money. The classic example is when parents of financial means manipulate their children with material things to influence their decision-making. And their largest threat is that of "cutting them off". Or, are you a woman or man coercing a relationship by buying someone off? Again, these are signals for change, and **supporting the notion of spiritual development will bring awareness, resolution, and management of those insecurities.**

A lack of personal growth most assuredly will affect the

body and mind, and will spill over into the types of relationships you select. For instance, you may have been trained to pursue a "socially" acceptable partner for marriage. Perhaps the one you love is not quite right in that department. If you begin to pursue a partner you know will meet the approval of family or friends, it will cost you dearly down the road in life. Initially, it will feel wonderful; all of those from whom you seek approval are flattering your choice. Then, the reality of living together sets in to remind you that your partner doesn't really have much in common with you, does not share the same goals in life—except for social status. When children are involved, this error is even costlier. Will you look to spirit to help pave a smoother road in your life?

The unrestricted energy of our spirit flourishes in all things positive, and equates to a magical *je ne sais quoi* in life. It is the kind of energy that is intuitive, and knows which way to go, and what to do—and most assuredly, takes us by surprise. Do you ever find yourself doing something unexpected that you might initially have thought about and dismissed as unrealistic? Have you ever had a feeling that is powerful enough to draw you into the consideration of things or people that you never thought possible? That's our spirit, our life IQ, our internal compass that can successfully steer all that we want in life—and sometimes, whether we like it or not, grabs hold and takes us there, despite the "kicking and screaming" of our physical and rational selves. Know that the ways of spirit do not always make sense. Generally speaking,

spirit does not conform to your timetable, and it doesn't present only *your* idea of opportunities.

When that happens, it usually feels like events and circumstances become unpredictable, disruptive, and sometimes crazy—regardless of our careful planning. This is why most times we will reject the calling of our spirit. We become desperate to maneuver things back to the way they were—the predictable way. However, this influential force will continue to make us feel like things aren't where they should be, aren't going right, and will make things downright difficult. Spirit makes us re-evaluate what we have been doing our entire lives. This fear, along with the unknown, can terrify us out of living life. **In accepting spirit, we must accept the unknown, and learn that the unknown cannot be controlled** with our well-formulated rationale and outright denial.

THE COMPOSITION OF SPIRIT

The phenomenal energy of our spirit is the energy of pure love. The feeling of love is so intangible a feeling, yet we all are pulled strongly in the continued search of this emotion. It is our natural way of being—to search for who we are. **This lifetime search represents how we learn to love.** Many times, our spirit is blocked by physical realities that dictate illusion and images of love, that fall very short of the real thing. Our definitions of love get skewed and go awry. Conditioning wrestles with our vulnerabilities, and takes us on a bumpy ride. However, the feeling of love is totally based on faith (just like spirit), of what we believe we are. Regardless of how love is inspired, we choose to believe that we love or are loved—and that—already makes us more spiritual than we think.

What, then, is the composition of our spirit? Our spirit is made solely of love, so there isn't a single material thing on which it thrives—or desires. **Our spirit is a kind of love absolute**. That means love in totality, love complete—not fragmented or conditional. To understand love, without conditions, we would have to consider that this type of energy would link itself to the energy of faith and hope. Why? Faith is the ability to trust. Trust is natural confidence. There is a sense of assurance and reliance—in this case, of YOU and who you are. Hope is acceptance—the acceptance that YOU are safe and unthreatened. When you live in spirit, you accept that what will come will be better for you. Then, hope manifests as pure optimism, and awakens our potential and all possibilities. When we love, and live in love, we experience compassion. It is the ability to understand. In this understanding, we gain wisdom—the attainment of insight. How many of us are truly striving to live this flawless energy every day?

We all are challenged to work on some aspect of love. **Developing our spirit means developing our ability to love.** In its natural state, love has no boundaries, is free, and can heal whatever ails us. Love disseminates all that is positive, including peace and tranquility. It inspires, motivates, and challenges us to become better. **Love, and the feeling of love, are powerful**

and overwhelming, and have no expectations. It then stands to reason that when engaging the physical world, love gets mangled by physical realities (expectations). These realities merely reflect *OUR* subjective view of life, and *if* at all negative, they will disassemble love, and cause us to question its value. We should not question love, but instead, our own value system and inability to accept the one thing we keep looking for. Is your definition of love congruent to what love really is?

The unspoiled energy of spirit has the ability to organize itself effortlessly, with or without our consent. Just like our body and our mind, our spirit also is made up of those subatomic particles. Whatever our true dreams and goals, those desires are getting organized, and continue to propel spirit to our desired direction, whether we acknowledge it or not. If we do not participate, we may not like the decisions of our spirit. When unconscious, this process takes a lot longer because we are busy facing countless difficulties. These difficulties generally represent resistance; the unwillingness to cooperate and align with spirit. These are the moments when we know very well what to do, or which action to take, *YET*, we forgo that initial instinct. Perhaps we think this instinct is crazy, or instinctive choice is too unrealistic to implement. We reject it. Maybe we are just afraid, and convince ourselves that it won't make a bit of difference. Why create negativity through resistance, and perpetuate unnecessary struggles and complications, when all we have to do is trust long enough to "let go" into our inherent energy source? It is frightening to trust something intangible, but rather than being unconscious in this process, why don't we try to participate consciously and align ourselves with spirit to foster the lives we want? **We need to learn to trust spirit.**

PRACTICAL WAYS TO NURTURE SPIRIT

First and foremost, **treat the energy of your spirit as something sacred**. It is special, and like no one else's. Spirit is a healing force that thrives on the integrity of self. If we operate without integrity, our reality becomes one of deceit and dishonesty, inviting complications and unnecessary difficulties. That struggle repels all things positive—particularly what it is we want most. The integrity of self is achieved through basic spiritual practices, and like everything else that we do in our life; an unshakable commitment must be made to spiritual development. **Integrity is being honest, truthful, and upright with our thoughts, intentions, and actions**. If we do our best to apply this discipline, we can count on our spirit's help to put into motion all the success we might ever imagine.

The process of **spiritual development** is not some magical awakening that just hits you one day down the road. It **requires change and changes**, and at first, might be difficult to practice regularly. We all have developed some bad habits and attitudes over the years. The good news is that there is a very big chance that you have been practicing one or more disciplines without realizing its positive impact on your life. For instance, you may be one who gives without expectations of receiving, and you do it all day long. You might have a way about you that accepts people, circumstances, or events the way they are. Or, you might be one that detaches from daily annoyances, relinquishing judgment, and going on your merry way. We will review basic spiritual practices that with time, will direct the energy of spirit toward the success and quality of living you desire.

Let's review and define the integrity of our thoughts, intentions, and actions. Thought is born from our desires. Intention is the ability to influence our desire, and that intention transforms the energy of our desire by "putting things into motion"—consciously or not. Action is the moment we have prepared for and are ready to act when opportunity presents itself. **All three are energy sources of significant magnitude**. The only difference is how quickly their power manifests. Many times, we consider a bad or negative thought as only a thought that no one knew—as long as we didn't act on it, all was OK. Not so. Since thought is where desire originates, that energy must expend itself somewhere. It might be a very small amount of negative energy, but it doesn't just disappear. Let's say our desire is to have revenge on someone who wronged us, or someone who wronged someone we love. Although time diffuses our original thought of revenge, the thought was transformed into negative intention. We may have pondered many ways to have revenge before we dismissed the plan completely. We did not act, but the energy force that we released into the energy of the entire universe, parked itself next to our name.

What does that really mean? It means that over time, if we continue a negative pattern of thinking, situations and circumstances will present themselves that will mirror our desire, or built-up desires. In this case, revenge. The energy of revenge comes together into a cluster of negative energy. Although, we may no longer desire to act with revenge, we will invite those who will take revenge on us—even if circumstances appear completely innocent. It will not matter if we did nothing to inspire revenge, the energy buildup already was there, and we will have to deal with it. Have you ever had the type of experience where you stood in astonishment because a complete stranger reacted angrily toward you? And all you did was excuse yourself when reaching for some fruit in a supermarket? What all of this means, is that we invited a complication or difficulty into our lives that could have been avoided if we paid better attention to the quality of our thoughts, intentions, and actions.

The same principle holds true, if in your mind, you always wish others well—no matter who they are. In that moment, you expend positive energy of thought that is influenced with the intention of wishing them well. You may not take action, to hold their door, help with groceries, but in your mind, you sent "positive" energy their way. All of that energy gets parked next to your name, as well. Why does that matter? That credit, so to speak, may be all that is necessary to secure a job you really had no chance of attaining, or by some strange miracle, you were alerted out of your bed, just in time to avoid a fire and deadly smoke inhalation—or, even more intangibly, the life of a loved one was saved.

Do not underestimate the power behind positive and negative thought, intent, and action. Action clearly has the most instantaneous reaction and results, but one never knows exactly how any energy—or group of energy—will be released. Do your best to **TAKE RESPONSIBILITY for all of your thoughts, intentions, and actions.** It is the beginning of taking charge of who you are. Whatever is happening, eliminate the pointing of the finger at things or people to blame for undesirable results. Know that you, and you alone, have the power to change it all—and that does not mean that you will change those people or circumstances, but you certainly will change the impact of that experience. Will you choose positive or negative? Recognize that this is the moment where you have an opportunity to create better experiences.

Many of you may have ascertained that the preceding stems from the spiritual law of justice—the law of karma. It is the natural principle of cause and effect. In Newtonian physics, it is the law of motion—that every action has an equal and opposite reaction. On an individual level, it means that we all carry (within our spirit) the cause and effect of all that we live, both positive and negative. The understanding of Karma encourages awareness that develops a regard for how we think and react—and as a result, how we treat others. This law can be used to free our mind from resentment, anger, and all things negative. Applying the principle of Karma and using a conscious effort when making choices, also can liberate us from feelings of victimization. Our thoughts, intentions and actions do matter—and when used in a positive way, we end up contributing to, rather than contaminating the environment around us.

There is a domino effect with spiritual practice. Regardless of order, all practices domino into one another. These spiritual laws thrive on each other to perpetuate a unity of energy with all that we do. If our choice is positive, we begin to draw upon that energy toward the successes we desire. One important note: Don't get caught up in all of the bad thoughts, intentions, and actions you may have participated in over your lifetime. Self-pity and beating yourself up only stagnates energy, in this case negative, making it even harder to dispose. It is more important to *shift* new energy in positive directions starting *NOW*. Learn from past mistakes, and permanently let them go.

Practice patience. As mentioned before, patience provides us with clear thinking, and the time to know ourselves. It inspires faith, and equips us with the type of endurance and persistence necessary to achieve what we desire. Practicing patience also invites the calm assessment of circumstances and events around us. It keeps us from making negative assumptions and conclusions through relaxed and peaceful investigation.

Practice acceptance. Like it or not, we need to accept that people, circumstances, and events are what they are. We may not like it, we may not agree, and we might feel terribly uncomfortable with this reality. However, know that when you impose YOUR view, standard or perspective on something or someone that simply *is not* of your perspective, you summon the forces of resistance. Undoubtedly, this will hold you back from anything that you desire. Accept people, circumstances, and events, as they are—not how you want them to be. That covers everything that we do in life, including how we pursue our relationships.

Accepting things as they are does not mean that you relinquish what you want. Let's say, you're looking for the love of your life. Although it is a fine desire, recognize the following: Continue to desire the love of your life, but let go of what it should look like, or who it might be. You might be so stuck on a particular trait or traits, that you block someone who just might be perfect for you. **Ask for what you want, but relinquish how it will be packaged**. The same holds true for your professional life. Ask for the job of your dreams—just let go of how it will come to you. The job of your dreams may have been visualized as one thing, while a job you least expected ends up bringing you all that you truly desired.

"Let go" and practice detachment. Begin by

practicing patience, which is the ability to detach from small annoyances, disruptions, and insecurities. Patience keeps our path in life uncluttered, less anxious, and trains us to detach from expectations. You might wonder how it is possible to detach from our expectations, particularly when deep emotions are involved, such as when you're in love. **Detachment is a type of letting go, not of your desire or emotion, but of the expectations or standards you impose on all that is happening to you.** It means you let go of negative feelings (insecurities) that cause you to "attach" and fester in that feeling. That festering pushes you toward building an expectation from events or from people.

Ask the question: "Is my life driven by need?" If one dissects the definition of need, it basically amounts to a requirement, prerequisite, or "must have". Then we can say that needs equate to expectations. **Expectations can be the disastrous end to what we truly want.** Sound crazy? Not really. We all have some sort of requirements and expectations in life; otherwise, how would we make decisions? The distinction *Your Life IQ* makes is to pay very good attention to your expectations, and how strongly you impose them into your life. They can make us chase something that will not make us happy, and can quickly extinguish the achievement of what we want in life. How? **Expectations are just needs packaged by fear, to limit what we can have in life**. Our desire is to control all that happens to us, so we don't have to feel uncomfortable, hurt, or vulnerable.

Let's say that you tend to struggle with not feeling good enough. Knowingly or not, you require external things to validate your feelings of inadequacy. You may place expectations on your loved one to acknowledge every little thing you do, searching for praise, and when it's not given, you feel offended, or assume that you are not appreciated. You might even get angry. These insecurities manifest as justifiable expectations that might not be met by the opposing person or circumstance. You then close the door unnecessarily, simply because *your* expectation was not met. Was that expectation worth an argument, or the possible loss of that relationship, or circumstance? Did you miss an opportunity because of your own inflexibility?

When you detach from expectations, you automatically accept a person or circumstance, and then there is nothing to deal with—except that person or circumstance. You end up making the most of that situation because it is not coated with your experiences from the past. The energy is free and uncomplicated. There is no struggling with how you want it to be versus how it is. It is the beginning of putting into motion all that you might ever want. For instance, you accept the circumstance that you were passed over for the promotion for which you had waited and worked for five years. Rather than belaboring how that could have happened, and how the person who aced the job got it, you begin to spend time on where else you might find the opportunity you originally wanted. It may have been that you never considered leaving the organization that you worked for, believing that it was the best you could attain. But now, because of that new circumstance of not receiving the promotion, your mind has opened up to the new possibility of going elsewhere to attain the job of your dreams. Which situation would you prefer to be in—the one where you dig yourself into a hole of defeat with no options, or the one with endless possibilities?

When you practice patience, then raise it a notch to detachment, the practice that follows will be total surrender. Surrender is a complete letting go; an action of giving into, submitting, and yielding to a higher power. That could mean the forces of the universe, or God, or, whatever or whomever you believe is a higher power. **When you acknowledge a higher power, a power higher than you, a type of humility is bred into all that is unknown**. In other words, you trust that you cannot control everything and its outcome, acknowledging there are other forces at work that just cannot be explained. You spare yourself the wrestling of trying to understand all that happens. Instead, you utilize and turn that energy into knowing that all that comes will be best for you—and you believe it. And why should we even consider such thinking? Take a look around. Does everything on this planet make sense to you? Does life unfold in a way that is predictable? Even if some of us believe we have a handle on what's going on, unpredictable events are guaranteed to affect us. It is a natural law of life.

It's worth noting that you are not alone if you believe in

a higher power. More than 9 out of 10 Americans still say, "Yes" when asked the basic question, "Do you believe in God?" This is down only slightly from the 1940s, when Gallup Polls first asked this question. Whatever you believe, whether in God, a higher consciousness, or other spiritual beings and masters, our spirit is the higher self—the one that is capable of connecting to more than just the physical and material life. The higher self has the ability to connect to metaphysical realities, and what some may call ethereal. So, however we define our higher power, know that it cannot be accessed without going through YOU first. We need to learn how to *talk* to the higher self. It's about getting comfortable in the unknown, and sometimes, what you simply cannot understand. **Not knowing, not anticipating, and not calculating, is the art of no control.** If successfully practiced, the art of no control allows for a steadiness that reaches our inner wisdom. Meditation and prayer is a fine practice to consider in order to achieve this goal. What is that inner wisdom? It is the wisdom that pops up during moments when you *just know* something is true, real, or right. They are all of those "light bulb" moments that magically appear over a lifetime. Your gut instincts also are first-hand advice sourced by your spirit.

Having a desire, and trusting the outcome to be best for us, is a powerful discipline. It maneuvers positive energy to manifest the things that we want. We open ourselves to all possibilities, and that gives us "the best odds," so to speak. **It is in the unknown where we are truly safe, without threat, and free**. Conditioning has imposed onto our thinking that all must be physically explained and tangible, including all of our ideas and feelings. Yet the continued evolution of mankind demonstrates that despite progress and advances, we still are beholden to things unexplainable. Why exert precious energy to fight it?

Letting go into the unknown is a practice that does not *force* anything. When we force solutions or expectations on people, circumstances, or events, we only create new problems. The ability to hand yourself over to the unknown creates a confidence that all will be worked out for the best, even if we don't know how. **Have all the dreams you want, but do not attach yourself to any type of expected results**. To be clear, this doesn't mean that you create a dream, and then do nothing else. Visualize as much as you want, but you will have to take each new step into the unknown by taking action until the next step surfaces. For instance, if you believe that you want to write a book, sit down and start writing. Even if you're not sure about how many characters are required for that story, or how many chapters you will have, just write. After a while, other ideas will enter your head that will confirm the next step. The appearance of the next step is guaranteed—provided you first take action.

Disengage from bad emotional habits. Although this discipline was covered in the chapter of *Mind*, complement the disengagement of bad emotional habits by **choosing COMPASSION over JUDGMENT.** Judgment is a bad emotional habit, and seems to be a national pastime. Whether we engage in judgment with people we know, or of celebrities and those we do not know, we're all doing it. What exactly is judgment? Judgment is when we rush to conclusions (usually negative), or when we are busy making hasty comments about people and/or their circumstances. We've all done it, but how often are you preoccupied with this activity? Know that when you indulge in jumping to negative conclusions about people and/or their circumstance, it is a sure way to block the power of spirit.

Habitual negative assumptions merely reflect a dissatisfaction of self. Let's be honest. When we are happy, it doesn't even occur to us to bother and talk about others negatively—we're too busy being happy. Choose compassion over judgment. Next time you see some grimacing waiter who crabbily asks for your order, rather than assuming you know the negative reasoning behind his mood that inspires you, to perhaps tell him off, choose the positive. Imagine that his wife died earlier that morning and he is at work because he cannot afford to lose a dime of his earnings because he has two children to feed. Without a doubt, you will feel compassion, and overlook the fact that he is grimacing and acting crabbily.

Judgment also manifests through other types of behavior and reactions. Is your reaction one of suspicion, or a feeling of threat? If we are mistrustful, we think others cannot be trusted, and usually feel threats and threatening situations around us. Can you distinguish negative emotions that cloud your perspective into judging others? If you are not quite sure as to why you exercise these negative habits, simply tell yourself over and over NOT TO HAVE THAT REACTION. Stop yourself, and choose compassion, even if you have to make up some crazy compassionate explanation as to why someone is the way that they are. **Don't be negative!** Even if you are *right* about someone's motivation or circumstance, you need to think about why you possess a need to repeatedly vocalize that you are right, rather than simply letting it go. Over time, you will develop **the discipline of tolerance** for those who may not understand as much as you, who may not see as you see, and you will begin to accept that we all face our life challenges in different ways.

Choose forgiveness, and know that absolutely everything is forgivable. Forgiveness is not about morality. Forgiveness is the ability to have mercy or pity on others and their behavior. This ability then leads to a kind of pardon and absolution of their transgression. Think about it. It doesn't mean that you suddenly say or think it's OK for what they have done. It just means you consciously put aside the *righteousness* that you might impose into your own life that will allow negativity to linger. Express your righteousness as you see fit, but remember to let it go.

Forgiveness does not always mean that we "kiss and make up," either. There are circumstances where we no longer can integrate that person into our lives because of toxic reactions that have no resolution, and they begin to affect us negatively. Perhaps the person was one of circumstance only, and besides that circumstance, we no longer have a connection. Regardless, forgiveness means the letting go of the negative emotions that keep us engaged with a circumstance and/or person, or repetitive negative thinking. **In forgiving, we let go of anger, pride, judgment, and even hatred,** so that our lives can once again be filled with the wonder of our spirit. In this wonder, there is grace. We consciously chose love so that we can dispense with a negative mindset. A positive byproduct of forgiving is that we are then able to release negative karma.

Sometimes family and loved ones are the most difficult to forgive and to let go of. Not all of us have had blessed circumstances with our family and loved ones. Some of us have been victims of violence, incest, and abuse, or have known loved ones to be victims of violence, incest, and abuse. All of these circumstances are life changing and difficult to resolve. Our conditioning and early childhood bonding is difficult to unravel, particularly with horrific events that have trained us into believing that we are unworthy. It is not an easy step to forgive, let alone move away from those that have hurt us. However, we should try to remember that challenging ourselves to forgive unleashes the purest of spiritual energy that can heal all that ails us. Remember that spiritually, we are equal, and that equality means that we are flawless and blessed. It entitles us to be the best we can be, and deserving of great things. Difficult as it may be, happiness, success, and love always is a choice. Will it be yours?

Live in the present. When you are a victim of your past, or a slave to your future, your spirit is unable to create new and thriving circumstances. You may have new circumstances in your life, but inevitably, your unresolved past or anxious future will get in the way by threatening what is new, and in the present. For instance, if you found a new love, but have unresolved feelings of unworthiness or inadequacy because of any wrongdoing from a past relationship, you bolt the door to possibilities. You will project that dissatisfaction and/or anger into your new relationship, in a way, you will be looking for reasons why it will not work, rather than looking for what will work—without the prejudice from the past. This prevents the success of that relationship in the future. If you have anxiety about your future, it is difficult to enjoy the present completely, and you may miss other opportunities that are happening in the present—because you are preoccupied with the future. Finding balance through personal growth that includes spiritual development will continually draw you closer to the here and now—by eliminating all that is negative and unresolved. Maintaining equilibrium by exercising body, mind and spirit, is a sure way to achieve success, and experience optimal well-being.

Choose love. In all that you do, choose love. With every thought, intention and action, are you posturing with love or fear? Know that there is no in between. The choice is either love or fear, and if that seems too simplistic, keep filtering your thoughts until you understand why it is fear that holds you back through inflexibility. Go back into the section of *Mind* and review, how fear manifests. **Choosing love means we begin to think of others and their feelings, along with ours, to build the integrity of the self.**

Who we believe we are is how we live and love. If who we are has not been evaluated and worked on, our defenses, facades, and other external behavior will be the navigator in life. We will be angry, fearful, aggressive, or dissatisfied. Our lives will be confused and riddled with our defenses, overreactions, and twisted communication of what and how we actually feel.

There are more than a hundred spiritual laws that have been in existence for thousands of years. They include some of the more familiar ones like the Law of Karma and the Law of Attraction. There are others that are not as well-known such as the Law of Vibration, the Law of Responsibility, the Law of Materialism, the Law of Grace, the Law of Good Will, the Law of Gender, and the list goes on. You might consider investigating these laws because they undoubtedly will reveal a connection that our world, its morality and value system, and standards are based on this knowledge. It reveals the powerful understanding available from spirit—and we all have it! Be conscious that a fragmented approach to spirituality is the same as a fragmented approach to your body health. It's all connected; separating and focusing on one law for too long without the practice of others, will stagnate your growth. You will discover that all thought can be conscious, and our special identity can develop freely as we tap into our intuition, our own special life intelligence. **Our life IQ gives us the right to develop our identity**—separate from conditioning, so that we do not depend on what others think. This IQ allows us to trust and have faith in who we are, and thus, allows us to filter out what we truly believe. This sacred approach directs us toward life fulfillment. Living a fulfilled life requires giving—expanding yourself in order to be able to give more of you, the true you, which is the foremost way to experience more out of life and people. Spiritual practice expands where we are today, and allows us to give more of who we are. **The giving of the self opens the heart and soul.** With this approach, you are able to attain success by receiving from everything around you.

ASKING FOR WHAT YOU WANT

This discipline is straightforward: Practice controlled breathing and center yourself. Go to that place where you are unencumbered by everyday realities—go into the silence of your mind and ask. Or if you prefer a house of worship, a park, or a beach, go there. Remember, it is imperative to slow down stressful and emotional moments that blur the realities of daily living with the intangible, spiritual realities of desire. Ask for whatever it is you want, and ask for guidance. Make sure you believe it with all of your might. Visualize it in any way you want. Write it down if this suits you. **Be strong, positive, and certain**. From that day forth, continue to ask for what you want, say it with strength, positivity and certainty. Every time you think of what you want, be strong, positive, and certain**. Detach from the result of how it will come, eliminate time, conditions, and expectations!** Remain flexible. Know that you can change and adjust that desire. Most of all, do not allow others to influence your choices. Keep those to yourself, if you have to. That's it, but you must continue the lifelong discipline of maintaining balance in all three components of body, mind and spirit. Sorry, everybody—there are no short cuts. There will be those who manifest a dream faster than you, but manifesting your dreams is not about speed. Know that many unknown circumstances are at play, and that it is not possible to control outcome.

The process of asking is the beginning of validating who you are. It is an action of humility where you respect and understand that you are a valuable participant in this world. Our spirit is free and not compromised. Nothing is forced. Your job is to make a commitment to being the best you can be. **Choose to behave in the spirit of integrity**. Take responsibility for all of your thoughts, intentions, and actions. Accept people, events, and circumstances—don't resist, and accept things as they are. Practice patience and discipline. Detach from conditions and expectations. Let go into the unknown, which will keep you living in the present. Choose compassion over judgment.

Tolerate all that you understand and all that you don't understand, and forgive the people around you. Do not try to convince or persuade others of what you believe is best for you, and in all that you do, choose love.

Become accustomed to asking for what you want. Make it a ritual. Ask for guidance. Be patient, flexible, and adapt to circumstances. We are spirit, and we are deserving of its power. **Spiritual discipline develops our ability to love, and it is the honor code by which we live.** We learn to relinquish control and to relish in the unknown. We do not anticipate, calculate, or expect. When spirit is developed, we feel enthusiastic, invincible, and free. The result is that we fall in love with life and all of its possibilities.

Will you choose or reject to live in spirit?

VI.

LIVING THE EXTRAORDINARY

In the Twenty-first Century, there is no escaping a mindset of big picture thinking. The entirety of what makes this world our world, has reached a global, all inclusive perspective. When we look to improve economic, social or environmental conditions, we now consider worldwide responsibility. Shouldn't we then consider that we have a duty to implement the same holistic thinking when it comes to the betterment of who we are? And, aren't we responsible for our own individual caretaking while searching for better life experiences?

As demonstrated throughout this book, each of us has a field of energy that is multi-dimensional—body, mind and spirit. We are a dynamic system of holistic energy, that when balanced, becomes a vibrant arena of strength and certainty. All of our individual energy sources overlap to create an energetic interdependency that fosters optimal experiences. It is the complete big picture point of view—a beneficial and empowering way to live—and it takes a positive shift in consciousness. Realizing that we, as human beings, possess a robust field of energy that can be developed and accessed as a reliable tool is awe-inspiring.

To live this remarkable truth, we must make a lifelong commitment to expand our knowledge, skills and practices. This approach means we dedicate ourselves to evaluations where we dare to ask the uncomfortable questions about how we live—and find the courage to change and step into the unknown. Big picture thinking encourages us to deliberate many more options, and eliminates myopic perspectives when facing adversity. It is the acceptance of a dynamic system in which our whole is greater than the parts. To experience the world with a holistic approach, and to achieve ultimate well-being, we are required to adapt throughout the many stages of life. It is a gratifying experience of expansion and growth.

It's a way of living that rejects a fragmented point of view because that attitude produces splintered results—results that are temporary, and many times, keep us spinning out of control. When we see our challenges through multiple prisms, multiple solutions exist. If we truly pursue a life where we seek meaning and fulfillment, and the desire to advance our wellness, we cannot avoid big picture thinking. In accessing and developing the extraordinary ability of your life IQ, and to integrate the energy of body, mind and spirit—a complete consciousness of living—is to experience the wonder in all that is life.

Our perceptions need to expand to understand how all energy contributes to how we live, and why *that* needs caretaking. Understanding that there are several variables to being healthy and living a fulfilled life will cause us to stop and think to make better choices. These decisions will be informed and optimal, thus advantageous when achieving our goals. But you're not alone if you struggle to elevate your standards. Our society continues to reinforce quick fixes to appease an immature perspective that doesn't want to do the work. We have fallen prey to "hyper realities," leaving us in a state where we need to feel instant gratification. This rush to a "high" leaves us perpetually dissatisfied and defeated, and has trained us to seek higher highs.

Life can be an extraordinary high when your field of energy clicks into a flawless type of perspective that imposes the feeling of being alive and happy. Evaluating all that makes us *alive* will determine how much meaning and happiness we experience while on the road of life. Changing beliefs expands awareness so that we plainly see our attitudes and values—to reveal those that no longer serve the success we desire. Positive change brings us closer to balance because we begin to live our truth. Our truth puts us at peace. We can do better than what society preaches, and we consciously can choose not to be limited. Have we had enough of life fatigue and powerlessness? Our life IQ gives us the right to seek fulfillment. Will you align who you are and what you want, with what you live? **Do you love yourself enough to change?**

The Wisdom of Balance

Balance exists when we change. This remarkable discipline rewards us with steadiness, focus and clarity.

We learn to navigate our lives effectively, particularly when we face unexpected and prolonged difficulties like unemployment, health crises and personal loss. But how is it that we learn? It is through the experience of an opposite, or an opposing side of what we desire. For example, to know happiness, we must know sadness. To know pleasure, we must know pain. To experience victory, we must experience loss. Change is the only way toward balance, as we gain knowledge through experience.

Balance is where we find satisfaction and peace. Maintaining our equilibrium is a process of positive change, and as we evolve, so will the depth of our experiences. When we resolve our difficulties in a holistic way, meaning enters our life, and we become satisfied with what we live. There is a sense of peace. If we pursue the goal of balancing body, mind and spirit, we will possess a perspective that affords us the kind of outlook that allows all viewpoints—without making us feel that we must defend our perspective. Our fears begin to dissipate, along with our limitations, and we destroy the inflexible wall of denial that insists only one way exists. You live in a liberated state of being, because you live true to yourself—you honor who you are in all that you live. In the state of balance, we feel happiness.

We have the power to produce contentment. Our thoughts and emotions control our vision of life, and its possibilities. Imagine what happens when we loosen the boundaries of what we think and feel. We relinquish control, and our life view is one of infinite possibilities. Balance is a message of love because we begin to love ourselves enough to envision better possibilities. Our steady perspective removes the limitations of what we can think and feel and it is expressed equally. All perspectives matter, none are judged, and we can select what will serve us best. We live within the integrity of who we are, and we feel satisfied.

Each of us possesses a personal blueprint that allows us to become the architect of our life. When we strive for balance, we are gifted with the ability to navigate what ails us. Our problems become secondary, and they do not rule or define our existence. Instead, we focus on the possibilities, and we raise the bar out of the fragmented approach of limitations, and into the big picture perspective of powerful decision-making. This is our life IQ.

Our life IQ energizes what we live, and produces faith in who we are. It is self-reliance. You trust yourself and your ability to choose what is right. Trusting yourself allows dreams to intensify and flourish because you develop confidence in what you can achieve. When we are able to reveal our truest nature, when we are able to be who we really are, we experience the feeling of being alive. And because of our Twenty-first Century lifestyles, now more than ever, we need to utilize our life IQ.

How will you honor yourself?

Being who you are is the highest achievement you can attain in life. How we regard ourselves is how we will define life. Improving your life IQ is about developing a positive relationship with yourself during all life stages. It is the only way we are able to thrive and succeed at what we deem important. When we learn to love ourselves, we learn to love all of what life has to offer. This is how you honor your individual self. You respect your uniqueness and you develop the courage to be you, in order to experience your truest potential.

Courage is the "x" factor in life—and it is the ability to take action *despite* your fears. Courageous people are not unafraid. They are experts at defying fear, and each of us can produce the courage necessary to implement our desires. The valor of who you are is driven by esteem. How you respect and love yourself is what raises or lowers your esteem. It's your value system, and that inspires confidence. The stronger your esteem, the stronger your ability to be courageous. How you regard yourself is built through achievement, and when it comes to life, all achievements matter—but they must be those that are true to your heart. Until you are able to confidently express who you are, you will be dissatisfied—no matter what you have attained in life. If you do not improve and achieve higher possibilities that satisfy your version of what makes you happy, you have nothing to draw from, or fall back on, when you are facing adversity. That internal gap of not honoring your true self leaves you empty and unhappy—without positive accomplishments to remind you of who you are. Instead, you choose externals—the attainment of money, material things, and even people to demonstrate your value—but you are empty as ever. **Balance in self inspires life fulfillment**, no matter what we are looking for. If our lives are supported by our true selves, we develop the confidence to take action.

Trusting the *real* you and accepting that life is a classroom of learning, is how we get to know ourselves. Our response to challenges, victories, and interaction with all that is the world, is how we honor ourselves. A successful life is about how we make choices that serve who we want to be. The more we connect with this understanding, the more comfortable we are with living life in the unknown—the truest definition of what life is.

Anything is possible. Will you believe it?

NOTE TO READERS: *YOUR LIFE IQ* was written from a compilation of study and life experience. This work represents a synthesis of nearly forty years of learning and absorbing information from a variety of sources.

Natalia Alexandria

Your Life IQ

www.ingramcontent.com/pod-product-compliance
Lightning Source LLC
Chambersburg PA
CBHW070955040426
42443CB00007B/518